THOMAS JEFFERSON

THOMAS JEFFERSON

Father of Liberty

Jeri Chase Ferris

Carolrhoda Books, Inc./Minneapolis

For my husband, Tom, with love and appreciation for your advice and support in our mutual pursuit of history, truth, and happiness!

My special thanks to Dr. Joyce Appleby, President, American Historical Association; Dr. H. Viscount Nelson, Jr., University of California, Los Angeles; and Lucia C. Stanton, Director of Research, Monticello, for their invaluable advice and comments on this book; to Susan Stein, Curator, Monticello, for her lengthy interview; to the staff at Monticello and at the University of Virginia Library, Special Collections; and to Vicki Revsbech, my editor at Carolrhoda Books, who made sense of it all.

Maps on pages 32, 82, and 97 by Bryan Liedahl

Carolrhoda Books, Inc., c/o The Lerner Publishing Group
241 First Avenue North, Minneapolis, MN 55401 U.S.A.
Website address: www.lernerbooks.com

Library of Congress Cataloging-in-Publication Data

Ferris, Jeri.
    Thomas Jefferson : father of liberty / by Jeri Chase Ferris.
        p.   cm.
    Includes bibliographical references and index.
    Summary: A biography that describes the love of books and learning as well as the personal life and political career of the third president of the United States.
    ISBN 1-57505-009-9 (alk. paper)
    1. Jefferson, Thomas, 1743–1826—Juvenile literature. 2. Presidents—United States—Biography—Juvenile literature. 3. United States—Politics and government—1783–1809—Juvenile literature. [1. Jefferson, Thomas, 1743–1826. 2. Presidents.] I. Title.
E332.79.F47 1998
973.4'6—dc21   97-46039

Manufactured in the United States of America
1 2 3 4 5 6 – JR – 03 02 01 00 99 98

CONTENTS

Jefferson drafting the Declaration of Independence, 1776

INTRODUCTION

Thomas Jefferson changed the world, and he did it with a pen.

He wrote with goose quill pens, steel pens, and even glass pens. He wrote on paper, on notebook pages made of ivory, and (once) on birch bark.

He wrote notes about everything he saw, read, heard, and thought about. He wrote letters to his friends, to his family, to perfect strangers who wrote to him, and even to the czar of Russia. He wrote new laws and government documents. He wrote in French, Spanish, Italian, Greek, and, of course, English. He wrote hundreds and hundreds of words every day, for nearly eighty years.

In those days there were no computers or typewriters or even ballpoint pens—yet Thomas Jefferson wrote more words by hand than most people ever write with the most powerful computers. And many of those words aren't just ordinary words—they are the foundation of America's democracy.

Thomas Jefferson changed the world with his pen, *and* he was the first secretary of state, the second vice president, and the third president of the United States.

1

BOYHOOD

Thomas Jefferson was born near the Blue Ridge Mountains of Virginia on April 13, 1743, when the fruit trees and redbuds were in bloom. His two big sisters, Jane and Mary, were delighted with their red-haired baby brother. They did their best to help the house slaves and their mother keep up with him in the Jeffersons' sprawling wooden house on the large tobacco plantation called Shadwell.

Tom's mother, Jane, was from the wealthy Randolph family, a family that was important in Virginia society. Tom's father, Peter, was not from a rich or important family. The Jeffersons had come from Wales and had worked hard to succeed in the new land of America.

Peter Jefferson had chosen a good piece of the new land for his farm. Shadwell was on rich soil near the Rivanna River, tucked up close to mountains covered with forests of walnut, redbud, and cedar trees. Mr. Jefferson, like most Virginia landowners, owned black men and women as slaves to work on that land—for at that time in America, people from Africa were bought and sold as property.

When Tom was only two, he and his family moved seventy miles away to Tuckahoe, the plantation of a relative who had died. Tom's mother and father were to care for the dead man's three children and plantation until the children were old enough to care for themselves. (Tuckahoe's house was big enough for two families; Shadwell's house wasn't.) Fortunately, Tom's new house was a *very* big house, for soon there were seven children under Mrs. Jefferson's care, including Tom's brand-new baby sister, Elizabeth.

Mr. Jefferson managed both Tuckahoe and Shadwell, with the slaves and overseers (men in charge of the slaves) he had left at home helping him care for Shadwell.

Even with two plantations to manage, Mr. Jefferson kept a close eye on Tom's schooling and probably started him on his ABCs long before he was five years old. While he was still little, Tom learned to write small, clear letters so everyone could read what he had to say, and he learned to read so he knew what everyone else had to say. Since there weren't any public libraries at that time, Tom was fortunate that his father had a library of more than twenty books, including Shakespeare. By the time Tom was six years old, he had read all those books, including Shakespeare, and was starting on them again.

Tom's first school was a tiny one-room schoolhouse near the main house. He had to stay there all day, of course, even if he already knew everything the teacher was teaching. But one day when the teacher droned on and on, Tom tiptoed out the schoolhouse door unseen. He ran behind the main house, got down on his knees, squeezed his eyes shut, and prayed hard that school would soon be over. It wasn't.

Tom preferred to be with his father. Mr. Jefferson was not only smart, he was a giant of a man, and as strong as he was big. He was also busy. In addition to running two plantations, Mr. Jefferson helped make laws for Virginia as a member of the Virginia House of Burgesses. He was also a famous surveyor and mapmaker. In 1751, when Tom was eight, Mr. Jefferson and another surveyor, Joshua Fry, made the first map of the whole colony of Virginia, the largest of the American colonies.

Tom's father knew a lot of math, and Tom eagerly learned it all. He trailed after his father in and out of the stables, the blacksmith's smoky shop, and the harness rooms that smelled of leather polish. He learned how to survey land, draw maps, and keep accounts. He was a good hunter in the woods, a strong swimmer in the river, and an excellent rider on a fast horse—the faster the better. He already loved (and had to have) beautiful things, whether a small well-printed leatherbound book or a sleek bay horse.

Tom, his father, his mother, and his sisters all had work

to do on the plantation. But Tom could see that the people who were the slaves did the hardest work. Slaves took care of the horses and drove the wagons. Slaves planted the gardens and weeded the fields. Slaves picked the tobacco and corn and cotton. Slaves cooked the food and cleaned the house. A slave's children were slaves, too. Slave children didn't go to school—they worked.

Tom also saw white children copying the way adults treated slaves. If an adult ordered a slave about in a rude way, the child did the same. This looked so terrible to Tom that he remembered it all his life, and wrote about it when he grew up.

Tom had plenty of slaves at hand to do whatever he needed, whenever he wanted. But his father taught him something else. "Never ask another," he said, "to do for you what you can do for yourself."

After seven years at Tuckahoe, the Jefferson family returned to Shadwell. Nine-year-old Tom didn't go with them. Instead, his father sent him to the home of the Reverend William Douglas, not far from Tuckahoe, where Tom would have the best possible education. The Reverend Douglas was a Scotsman, a strict churchman and teacher, who started Tom on Greek, Latin, and French. Tom lived with the Douglas family (where, he said, he ate moldy pies) and went home to Shadwell for summer vacation.

Tom didn't waste a minute of summer. He rode over the plantation with his father. He roamed with his friends up and down the tree-covered Virginia mountains, always carrying his long gun in case he met a bear, a wolf, or a

Shadwell, birthplace of Thomas Jefferson. The house burned to the ground in 1770.

bobcat. He read and dreamed alone under the maples and dogwoods and chestnuts. He hunted and fished, he swam and canoed.

These happy, easy years ended when Tom was fourteen.

In August of 1757, Tom's tall and powerful father died. He had never been sick, he was only forty-nine, and suddenly he was gone. Now there was no man for Tom to model himself after, no man to guide him. Now Tom, a gangly, red-haired teenager, was responsible for his six sisters, his two-year-old brother, even his mother. He desperately missed his father. He felt entirely alone.

Tom's father left him what they both treasured most:

his books, his writing desk, and his surveying and drawing tools. To Tom and Tom's brother, Randolph, he left 7,500 acres of land, 200 hogs, 70 cattle, and 25 horses. He also left them 60 slaves. He left his 6 daughters some money and a slave apiece, and gave Tom's mother the use of her share of the house and farm for the rest of her life.

Tom would not inherit his share of the land and slaves until he was twenty-one. In the meantime, the overseers and slaves would work the plantation while Tom went to school. Five men, chosen by Tom's father, were to advise Tom's mother for the next seven years.

Tom had never really liked the cold-natured William Douglas (or his wife's moldy pies), and he had learned everything the Reverend Douglas had to teach him. So he began to study with the Reverend James Maury, who lived near Shadwell. Maury helped Tom understand Greek and Latin so well that he took notes from Greek and Roman philosophers in their own languages. In fact, Tom could read Greek, Latin, French, and Italian before he was twenty.

The Reverend Maury was a somewhat sour man, and his school was a log cabin, but he had a *huge* library of four hundred books. Tom devoured the words in those books as if they were sweet Virginia ham. He began to keep a notebook so he could write down favorite passages from books, or ideas he had while he was reading. He also practiced the violin, sometimes for three hours a day.

Now that Tom was close to home, he and his older sister Jane were often together, reading, singing, walking, and talking. Jane loved music as much as Tom did, and

Tom knew she also understood his passion for learning. She was a true friend.

Another friend, Dabney Carr, was a boy just Tom's age. They went to Maury's school together. In fact, they did just about everything together: they rambled through the woods, they rode, fished, and swam. But what they both liked best was to scramble up one wonderful mountain on Tom's land and lie under a huge oak tree at the very top to study or read or just talk. It seemed to Tom as though he could see the whole world from there. Tom and Dabney promised each other that the one who died first would be buried by the other under that oak tree on the top of that mountain. Of course, neither one expected to die for a long, long time.

In three years Tom learned everything the Reverend Maury could teach him (and read all his books). He enrolled at the College of William and Mary in Williamsburg, one hundred miles east of Shadwell.

In the spring of 1760 Tom rode into Williamsburg. He was seventeen. His slave Jupiter, also seventeen, rode with him.

Williamsburg was the capital of the colony of Virginia. The British royal governor of the colony lived there in an elegant English-style brick mansion surrounded by an English garden. A visiting Englishman would have felt right at home, for the American colonies did, after all, belong to England and England's new young king, George III.

Tom's friends John Page and Dabney Carr were at William and Mary, and so were many new friends. The

In 1760 Williamsburg was a small town of only one thousand people and two hundred wooden houses. The main street *(above)* was just one mile long, with the college at one end and the capitol at the other end. In between were boot makers, wig makers, silversmiths, chocolate shops, lace and ruffle shops, and lots of bookstores.

young men who attended William and Mary were almost all from rich, upper-class families. They each had a fine horse (at least one), a personal servant (at least one), and fancy clothes (plenty of them).

At first Tom spent a lot of money on silk stockings and fancy hats, and a lot of time dancing, singing, and flirting with the beautiful young women of Williamsburg. He spent many shillings at the coffeehouse and many hours in quiet conversation, his gray-green eyes warm and cheerful. He wasn't good at telling jokes, but he was a great violin player, a wonderful dancer, a steady friend, and one of the most likeable men in Williamsburg. And he came close, he said, to going off on the wrong track and becoming "worthless to society."

But three very different and very important men noticed Tom Jefferson. They saw something remarkable in this tall, thin, freckle-faced teenager with hair as red as autumn leaves.

One of these men was Tom's math, science, and philosophy teacher, William Small, who became "as a father" to Tom. Another was George Wythe, a brilliant lawyer, whom Tom soon called "a 2nd father." The third man was Francis Fauquier, the English governor of Virginia, a friend of Small and Wythe. These good men invited Tom to join their group, and a new world opened before him. Many evenings Tom dined on oysters and wild duck at the Governor's Palace, where he learned more about politics, philosophy, and science than he had ever heard in his life. These men, Tom said, "fixed the destinies of my life."

Dabney and John were amazed at the change in Tom. He started to get up at five o'clock every morning, and he began each day by putting his feet into a tub of cold water that Jupiter brought. Tom believed this kept him from getting sick. (It also woke him up.) Then he was off to his books: calculus, physics, natural science, agriculture, astronomy, chemistry, history, languages. He studied for hours—sometimes fifteen hours a day. He also ran two miles, rode his horse, and practiced his violin every day. He wrote in his notebooks constantly. He was a good listener and a caring friend. He even found time to fall in love.

George Wythe. When Wythe died in 1806 he left Tom his most valuable possession, his law library.

One of the most beautiful young women in Williamsburg was Rebecca Burwell, and she was Tom's choice. He wrote notes about the beautiful "R.B." to Dabney and John, but when he tried to say clever things to Rebecca herself, he stammered a few broken sentences and ended up not saying anything at all. He wrote romantic poems he didn't send and thought romantic words he couldn't say. To his great surprise, Rebecca married someone else. (Thomas Jefferson never did become a good speaker. He preferred to write.)

When he went home on vacation, he found that Shadwell was not the paradise it used to be. He missed his father. He wrote John that every single day was exactly like the one before it. "We rise in the morning that we may eat breakfast, dinner, and supper, and we go to bed again that we may get up the next morning and do the same. . . . you never saw two peas more alike than our yesterday and today." But at least his favorite sister, Jane, was there, and his mountain. Every summer evening he paddled his canoe across the Rivanna River and climbed that mountain in time to watch the sun set behind the blue hills and distant clouds.

2

A NEW FAMILY

Tom finished at William and Mary in the spring of 1762. Then he decided to study law with his friend George Wythe, the best law teacher in Virginia. Tom's notebooks overflowed with notes in five different languages about what he read, heard, and thought; and his shelves overflowed with books. "A lawyer without books would be like a workman without tools," he explained.

Tom turned twenty-one in 1764. Now he was responsible for the care of his family and his slaves, along with his law studies. He also had to make sure the work on his large farms was done properly while he was studying in Williamsburg. Those farms had to grow enough corn and tobacco to pay for everything his family and slaves needed.

About this time King George III, who was only five years older than Tom, decided to show his American colonies that he was a *real* king. He told his soldiers in America to look into people's houses and barns and stores and see if they were following all the king's rules. The colonists did not like this.

Then King George began to tax the American colonies

King George III of England, who was just twenty-two when he became king in 1760

under a new law called the Stamp Act. Whenever a person paid a bill, or bought a newspaper or a school book or any of fifty-two other things, there was a stamp tax to pay. The colonists did not like this at all.

The hated Stamp Act was repealed the very next year, but in its place were new taxes on English goods, such as glass, lead, paint, paper, and tea. These taxes were even worse than the Stamp Act, as Americans used these English goods every day; they had English habits and customs; they *were* English.

Life went on as usual, despite these worrisome taxes,

and Tom went home in July of 1765 for a joyous celebration. He stood happily with his sister Jane as their younger sister Martha married Tom's best friend, Dabney Carr.

Only ten weeks later, when Tom was back in Williamsburg, Jane died. Tom was stunned and heartbroken. "Ah, Jane, best of girls," he wrote in his notebook, "farewell for a long, long time."

Tom returned to Shadwell at the end of 1765 with his law degree and a heavy heart, and went to work organizing his farms. In the spring he began a new notebook, his Garden Book. On the first line he wrote, "Purple hyacinth begins to bloom." He wrote down when every flower came up, when and where he planted everything he grew (actually, Tom's *slaves* did the planting), and when the vegetables "first came to table." He wrote gardening tips ("40. f. square of watermelons will supply a family that is not very large"), farming tips ("8 or 10. bundles of fodder are as much as a horse will generally eat thro' the night"), and suggestions for the next year.

Tom had to have his thoughts, his feelings, and his possessions in order, all the time. Notebooks helped him do it. His notebooks were models of neatness and order, and he kept his quill pens sharp so he could get a lot of writing into a little space. In one book he kept notes about his reading; in another he kept his money accounts and lists of things to do. He wrote down the price of an egg; errands to run (remember to . . .); bills to pay (bought horse for £11 payable April 1); shopping lists (black silk stockings, knives and forks, jelly, scarlet cloth); reminders to

1774

May. 4. the blue ridge of mountains covered with snow.

5. a frost which destroyed almost every thing. it killed the wheat, rye, corn, many tobacco plants, and even large saplings. the leaves of the trees were entirely killed. all the shoots of vines. at Monticello near half the fruit of every kind was killed; and before this no instance had ever occurred of any fruit killed here by the frost. in all other places in the neighborhood the destruction of fruit was total. this frost was general & equally destructive thro the whole country and the neighboring colonies.

14. cherries ripe.

16. first dish of pease from earliest patch.

26. a second patch of peas come to table.

June. 4. Windsor beans come to table.

5. a third & fourth patch of peas come to table.

13. a fifth patch of peas come in.

July. 13. last dish of peas.

18. last lettuce from Gehee's/

23. Cucumbers from our garden.

31. Watermelons from our patch.

Aug. 3. Indian corn comes to table.

Black eyed peas come to table

Nov. 16. this morning the Northern part of the Blue ridge is white with snow.

17. the first frost sufficient to kill any thing.

A page from Jefferson's early Garden Book. All of Jefferson's notebooks were neat and orderly, filled with the ordinary notes of life.

himself (I have promised . . .). These notebooks were always in his pockets, and as soon as he did a thing on his list he crossed it off. Before the notebooks, Tom had often made notes on scraps of paper from his pocket to copy later, "which however they hardly ever were." Notebooks were better.

Tom took his first law cases in 1767. He rode about two hundred miles a month around the colony of Virginia, collecting information for his cases—and for himself—and writing it into his notebooks. (Jupiter rode with him to help carry things.) Tom met immigrants from Europe who were pouring onto the western frontier of Virginia, and he began to specialize in land law, as well as debt and divorce cases.

Tom's law career was underway. Now he began to think about building his own home on his own mountaintop, the one he and Dabney used to climb. Everybody said the right place to live was down by a river, where the water was, where barrels of tobacco were rolled right onto the ships. That's where the richer and flatter land was, too. That's where the roads were. Nobody should build a house on top of a mountain, they said. But Thomas Jefferson thought differently. Never mind that his mountain was a steep one with no water at the top of it. Never mind that there were no roads for horses to pull wagons up the mountain. Everybody else might build by a river; Thomas Jefferson would build on top of the world.

In 1768 he hired a workman to start leveling off the top of his mountain. This was the beginning of Monticello, which means "little mountain" in Italian. Tom used an

Italian word because he thought the Italian architecture he had seen in books was the most beautiful in the world, and he wanted his house to be beautiful. (He thought the typical brick or wood houses of Virginia, even the mansions in Williamsburg, were ordinary.) So he bought a book by Palladio, a sixteenth-century Italian architect, and began drawing plans for his house, his gardens, and all the extra buildings needed by a Virginia landowner: stables, kitchen, laundry, smokehouse, blacksmith, dairy. He drew in slave cabins, too, for the only way he knew to run a large plantation was with slaves. Still, he fretted about slavery.

Much later Tom wrote, "Nothing is more certainly

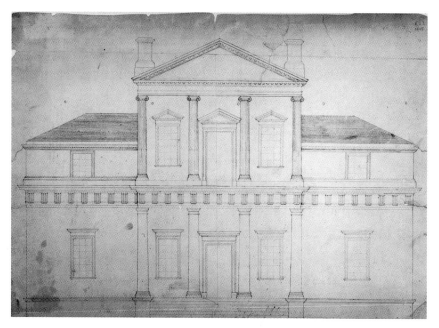

Jefferson's ink drawing of the first version of Monticello, 1771. It's not known if the second-story porch was built before he began building all over again.

written . . . than that these people are to be free." In the meantime, he tried to set an example of kindness to his slaves, directing them with courtesy and good humor. He also paid small salaries to his most valuable slaves. Thomas Jefferson's slaves lived better than most slaves—but they were still slaves.

In December 1768, twenty-five-year-old Thomas Jefferson was elected to the Virginia House of Burgesses, as his father had been. As soon as he was elected, he urged that Virginia slave owners be given the right to free their slaves as they chose. His suggestion was shouted down. Two years later Jefferson took the case of a slave who asked for freedom because his mother had been freed. In his argument before the court Jefferson said, "Under the law of nature, all men are born free." This was too much for the judge, who pounded his gavel furiously and refused to hear any more. Thomas Jefferson lost that case.

And in England, King George, who kept making mistakes about the American colonies, was on his way to losing *them.*

At the 1769 meeting of the House of Burgesses at Williamsburg, Tom Jefferson and the other burgesses passed some surprising resolutions. They said King George was wrong to tax his colonies and wrong to take "traitors" (Americans who disagreed with the king) to England for trial. When the new English royal governor heard these resolutions, he angrily ordered the burgesses out of the capitol and locked the doors.

So Thomas Jefferson, George Washington, Patrick

Henry, and others moved their meeting down the street to the Raleigh Tavern. They agreed to write to all thirteen colonies saying all the colonies should stick together. No one in America should buy anything more from England, whether candy or carriages, they said, until the king came to his senses. First, though, Tom ordered boxes of books about government to be sent to him immediately—from England.

That spring and summer at Monticello, Tom had his slaves plant pear, cherry, apple, peach, fig, and walnut trees. He had a long row of mulberry trees planted where the workshops for Monticello would be. He told his slaves to dig a well and, before the well was finished, he had them carry buckets of water up the mountain to water the trees. He had his slaves, and a brickmaker from Williamsburg, begin to make bricks from the red clay soil of his mountain. Things were going well.

The following February, while Tom was away, the Jefferson family home at Shadwell burned to the ground. Everything Tom owned, except for the notebooks he had with him, was in ashes, including the treasured books and desk from his father. (A slave saved Tom's violin.)

Fortunately, no one was hurt in the fire. Tom wrote a friend that he wouldn't have minded if it had been money he lost, but it was "every paper I had in the world, and almost every book." His mother, brother, and sisters moved to another Randolph plantation, and Tom rented rooms in Charlottesville. He paid his men extra to work even faster at Monticello.

Tom and his family were not alone in their troubles. In

Boston, people were protesting against King George and his taxes and his soldiers in their smart red coats. In March 1770, an angry group of men and boys threw snowballs at British "redcoats" marching down a Boston street. The redcoats fired back with bullets, killing five men. News of the Boston Massacre was carried south to the shocked citizens of Williamsburg by fast-riding horsemen.

Meanwhile, at Monticello Tom's slaves dug cellars and laid bricks. In October the first small, square one-room brick building was finished, and Tom happily wrote in his account book, "Moved to Monticello." At last he was living on his own mountaintop, just as he had always dreamed, with his gardens and fruit trees all around him. But something was missing, and Tom was lonely.

Then, in Williamsburg, he met Martha Wayles Skelton, a tall, graceful widow with a joyful personality and a three-year-old son. And Martha, like Tom's sister Jane, was an excellent musician. Tom promptly fell in love. He began buying theater tickets and fine clothes, hair powder and bright shoe buckles. He bought a large green silk umbrella for beautiful Martha, to go with her thick auburn hair and hazel eyes.

Tom's horse soon wore a path between Williamsburg and Martha's home, "The Forest," where she and her son lived with her father. Something about Martha's cheerful laugh and easy manner helped the shy Mr. Jefferson say the tender words he longed to say, and Tom and Martha soon knew that they wanted to be together for the rest of their lives. Next, Tom needed to convince Mr. Wayles,

Martha's wealthy father, that he was good enough for Martha.

But Tom was not the only man who thought Martha was special. One evening two other young men came to call on her. As they waited outside the parlor, hats in hands, they heard music and laughter. They put their ears to the door. Martha was playing the harpsichord and singing; Tom was accompanying her on his violin. The two young men looked at each other sadly, put on their hats, and left. Soon Mr. Wayles, too, was convinced that Tom was the man for Martha.

Tom and Martha were married on January 1, 1772, at The Forest, in the midst of swarms of relatives. Several days later they set out for Monticello, one hundred miles away. As they traveled, thick snow began to fall. By the time they reached the bottom of Tom's mountain the snow was so deep the horses couldn't pull the carriage. So Tom unhitched the carriage, and he and Martha jumped onto the horses' warm backs and rode bareback up the mountain in a snowstorm. Jupiter hadn't known when they were coming, so Tom's little brick house was dark and cold. But Tom soon had a fire going. He found a bottle of wine on the bookshelf, and he and Martha laughed and sang together at Monticello for the first time.

In September Martha and Tom's first baby was born, a strong and healthy girl. They named her Martha, for her mother, and called her Patsy so the two wouldn't get mixed up. (Martha's little son had died in 1771.)

When Tom went back to the House of Burgesses in the spring, he met the new royal governor for Virginia. Proud,

The first building at Monticello. Tom and Martha lived in this tiny house, cozy and warm, all winter.

haughty Governor Dunmore didn't think much of the American colonists. Tom didn't think much of Dunmore, either. Right under Dunmore's nose, Tom and his friend Dabney helped set up a new committee, called the "Committee of Correspondence," which would write to all the other colonies about King George's actions. This way the colonies could work together. Then they rode home, talking cheerfully over their horses' hoofbeats.

Dabney died in May. Tom was grief-stricken, but he remembered the promise they had made to each other. Dabney was buried under the great oak tree at the top of Tom's mountain. The inscription Tom wrote for

Dabney's gravestone ends, "To his virtue, good sense, learning, and friendship, this stone is dedicated by Thomas Jefferson, who of all men living, loved him most." Tom brought his sister Martha, who was Dabney's widow, and her six children to Monticello to live so he could take care of them.

That same year his wife's father died, leaving her 135 slaves, 669 books, 11,000 acres of land spread out over several farms, and a large debt. One of Martha's new slaves was Betty Hemings. Some of Betty's children were possibly the children of Martha's father. If so, they were Martha's own half sisters and half brothers—and her slaves.

Tom Jefferson, age thirty, was now responsible for the food, housing, and life of hundreds of people, mostly slaves, and for thousands of acres of farmland. He stayed at Monticello all fall and winter, directing his slaves as they made one hundred thousand bricks and planted the crops. He read and thought about the disagreements between the king of England and his American colonies. Who was right? What should the colonists do?

3

A NEW NATION

Many colonists were getting tired of asking King George to remove his soldiers and to stop taxing them on things they needed to buy from England. But it seemed that the more they tried to explain this to the king, the more the king's advisors told him to be firm and tough with the colonists.

So in December 1773, some of the angriest colonists dressed up as Indians, went to Boston Harbor, climbed onto the king's ships, and threw all the boxes of tea that were to be sold to the colonists (after they paid the taxes) into the water.

King George was not pleased when he heard about the Boston Tea Party, and his advisors told him to be firmer and tougher. The king sent a royal message that as punishment for this crime Boston Harbor would be closed on June 1, 1774, until every leaf of tea was paid for. This was bad news, indeed, for almost every single item the colonists sent to England or received from England came through Boston Harbor.

Tom heard the news in May, in Williamsburg. He and

his friends wrote a letter to all the colonies suggesting that they send delegates to a meeting to talk about what to do next. It was decided that the First Continental Congress would meet in Philadelphia in September. Tom was supposed to go, but in September he was at home, too sick to travel. He wrote down his ideas and sent his notes to the Congress in Philadelphia.

When the men at the First Continental Congress read Tom's notes, they shook their heads. And no wonder. Tom had written that the British king did *not* have the

THE THIRTEEN COLONIES

right to rule the American colonists. He'd written that the colonists themselves had fought for, died for, and conquered this land, and it was theirs. He'd written, "Kings are the servants, not the [owners] of the people."

This was going too far for most of the men in Philadelphia, who were still trying to come to an agreement with the king about his rules for America. Finally the congressmen decided that they must try to be at peace with the king. Most colonists did not want to fight the British army just because they disagreed with the king's taxes. But more and more colonists were also feeling less like British Americans and more like plain Americans.

Tom got well and happily stayed home with Martha, Patsy, a plump new baby named Jane, and his books. He made notes in his Garden Book, Farm Book, and account book. He read, wrote, and thought about America, about the king, and about slavery.

Meanwhile, Tom's slaves built brick walls and planted garlic, spinach, carrots, lettuce, raspberries, watermelons, and more trees, all as Tom ordered. Slaves and bricklayers tramped through the dirt and mud, making huge cellars for all the storerooms Tom planned to build. Tom showed them how to lay bricks exactly as he wanted, and he measured for new roads to be dug around his mountaintop. He rode around his different farms, talking to the overseers and slaves, checking the tobacco and corn. His farms had to make enough money to support his family and slaves, and build Monticello, too. Soon he was so busy with farming and politics that he gave up his law practice.

All over the thirteen colonies, people were still unhappy with King George's rules and taxes. In 1774 some Virginians had met to discuss the problems. Now, in March of 1775, there was a second meeting, to talk again and to choose delegates for the Second Continental Congress.

Tom went to the second Virginia Convention in Richmond. Peach trees blossomed sweetly outside the plain white church where 125 men argued loudly about whether it was time to fight back against their king, who was taking freedom after freedom from his American colonies. At last Patrick Henry stood and said, "There is no longer any room for hope. . . . If we wish to be free . . . we must fight! . . . Is life so dear, or peace so sweet, as to be purchased at the price of chains and slavery?" Tom held his breath as Henry cried, "Forbid it, Almighty God! I know not what course others may take, but as for me— give me liberty, or give me death!" The room was silent. The arguing stopped. Virginia, the largest colony of all, was for liberty. (A man in the crowd listening outside gasped, "Let me be buried at this spot.")

Delegates from all the colonies met at the Second Continental Congress that summer in hot and sticky Philadelphia, to "consider the states of America." Tom Jefferson was there as a Virginia delegate and met the famous Benjamin Franklin and John Adams. Short, prickly John Adams said of tall, amiable Tom, "He soon seized upon my heart."

Congress decided to have two committees: one to write a letter of reconciliation with England and the other to raise money to prepare for war in case the letter of reconciliation didn't work. The men agreed that the American colonies should be prepared to protect themselves against British soldiers, who were already fighting and killing Americans outside Boston. They chose George Washington, a quiet and honorable soldier and farmer, to be commander of the new American army.

Tom went home at the end of December. His baby daughter Jane had died in September, and he and Martha were still heartbroken. Then his mother died. Tom had a severe headache for weeks and didn't even write in his Garden Book. Things seemed very much out of his control.

King George was also out of Tom's—or any of the colonists'—control. The king rejected the colonists' letter of reconciliation and declared them rebels. General George Washington raised the new American flag for the first time on January 1, 1776, and in May 1776, the third Virginia Convention proposed that Congress declare the United Colonies to be free and independent states. Again Tom was needed in Philadelphia, and again he drove down his mountain in a carriage crammed with books. A young slave, Bob Hemings, drove another carriage filled with trunks and boxes.

As soon as they got to Philadelphia, Tom found a stable for his horses, a place for Bob, and a room for himself on the second floor of a three-story brick house on Market Street. Then he went to work with Congress.

Each day started with a hearty breakfast before work began in the meeting hall at ten o'clock. The president of the Continental Congress, John Hancock, would often open the session by reading the latest letter from George Washington describing the condition of his army (terrible). Tom listened, slouching sideways in his chair with his long legs stretched out, sometimes whispering to his neighbor. Although he was known for his clear thinking and precise speech when talking with two or three people, he seldom spoke out in a group. John Adams said he never heard Tom say three sentences together, which must have been a relief after hearing men who talked on and on without saying anything.

In June, Congress chose five men to write America's

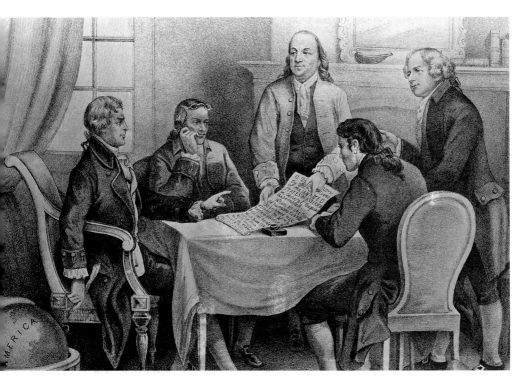

The committee chosen to write the Declaration *(left to right):* Thomas Jefferson, Roger Sherman, Benjamin Franklin, Robert Livingston, John Adams

The desk on which Jefferson wrote the Declaration of Independence. Jefferson drew a picture of the desk he wanted and a carpenter quickly made it. It was simply a box with a top that could unfold to make a large writing surface, and a drawer to hold paper, quills, ink, and sand to blot the ink.

declaration of reasons for fighting against England: Thomas Jefferson, Benjamin Franklin, John Adams, Roger Sherman, and Robert Livingston. Adams said Jefferson was the man to do the writing, as he had "a happy talent" with the pen. The declaration had to be clear, yet beautiful; simple, yet wise.

So, in his second-floor sitting room, Tom sharpened a new quill and began to write the paper that would explain to the whole world why England's American colonies were fighting to become free states. He needed every bit of knowledge he had gained in his thirty-three years, he needed a good desk, and he needed a lot of paper. Tom wrote and rewrote for seventeen days until he thought every word was perfect as "an expression of the American mind."

"When, in the course of human events," he began, "it becomes necessary for one people to dissolve the political bands which have connected them with another, . . . they should declare the causes which impel them to the separation.

"We hold these truths to be self-evident: that all men are created equal; that they are endowed by their Creator with certain inalienable rights; that among these are life, liberty, and the pursuit of happiness. . . ."

When the whole declaration was finished, Jefferson gave it to Adams and Franklin to read. They were pleased with its elegance and made only a few changes. But when the declaration was shown to the entire Congress on June 28, the idea that *people* make a government and that a king's people could decide they no longer wished to be ruled by him was still too shocking for some of the men. "This is treason!" they cried. Some believed it was a terrible mistake to leave the safety of English rule, to "burn down our house in mid-winter and have no other house to shelter us."

A fearful, quarrelsome Congress began ripping Tom's words to shreds. John Adams, Tom was glad to see, fought "fearlessly for every word." Tom himself did not argue—in fact he never argued, except with his pen.

Some of what Thomas Jefferson wrote was taken out, such as a long argument against the slave trade (some states would not have agreed) and the beautiful phrase of

Jefferson's rough draft of the Declaration of Independence, with the finished version inset. In Jefferson's rewriting, and in the final copy, "inalienable rights" became "unalienable rights."

regret to the king "we might have been a free & a great people together. . . ." But on July 2, Congress approved the Declaration of Independence. (They kept arguing about it for two more days, however.)

Also on July 2 a letter from General Washington arrived, saying that British warships were gathering off New York and he needed men and supplies *now*. (Congress kept arguing.)

On July 4, 1776, Tom recorded the temperature with a

The Declaration of Independence by John Trumbull. Jefferson helped Trumbull with this painting by describing the signing of the Declaration in detail and sketching the room for him. In the painting, Jefferson has unpowdered reddish hair and wears a vivid red vest. Left to right: John Adams, Roger Sherman, Robert Livingston, Thomas Jefferson, Benjamin Franklin.

new thermometer at 6 A.M. (68°), at 9 A.M. (72°), at 1 P.M. (76°), and at 9 P.M. (73°). He bought guitar strings and seven pairs of gloves for Martha, and put his notes in order.

That evening, the delegates walked one by one to the desk at the front of the hall and in silence signed their names to the Declaration of Independence. As Tom had written, by this declaration "we mutually pledge to each other our lives, our Fortunes, and our sacred Honour."

Now the men of the new United States Congress really had to get busy. They all knew that Benjamin Franklin was right when he said if they didn't all hang (work) together, they would surely all hang (by their necks) separately.

On July 8 the Declaration of Independence was read out loud from the yard of the State House in Philadelphia, and in every colony. Church bells rang. In big and little towns all over the colonies, men, women, and children shouted, "God bless the free States of North America!" Cannons roared in celebration, and men built bonfires in the streets, tore down the king's signs, and threw them into the flames. In New York City, crowds pushed over a lead statue of King George III and melted it into bullets to shoot at King George's soldiers.

And finally, Tom hurried home.

4

THE VIRGINIA YEARS

Red and gold maple leaves crunched under the carriage wheels as Tom drove eagerly up his mountain. Bird songs came from every tree, and a squirrel scampered up a nearby oak. This was where he wanted to stay, and where he was needed most. Martha was sick and still sorrowing over the death of their daughter Jane; he had to take care of business at Monticello; and he had work to do in his own state of Virginia.

Tom wanted Virginia to be a model for the new United States. This is the time to get things changed, he wrote, "while our rulers are honest, and ourselves united." He wanted Americans to have freedom to own land, freedom to worship or to not worship, freedom to learn. He wanted to open a free public library so anyone could borrow a book. He wanted talent and education to determine how far people could go in life, not how much money they had. He believed government should be ruled by the people, *educated* people. So he wanted free public schools. He wanted to begin to train slaves to work for themselves.

But his thinking jumped ahead of other people's. The new laws he wanted were not passed. (Not then, anyway. Some of them were passed ten years later.)

Jefferson helped elect Patrick Henry as the first governor of Virginia, and worked for three years with his old teacher George Wythe and others to rewrite the former English laws of Virginia. "The people will be happiest whose laws are best," Tom said.

Tom and Martha's first son was born in May of 1777. One month later the baby died. Tom stayed with Martha until the autumn leaves fell like rain, and he had to return to Williamsburg. Their fourth child, Mary (called Polly), was born the next August. They now had two children living and two dead, and Tom had no intention of ever leaving Martha again.

In June 1779, Thomas Jefferson was elected governor of Virginia. Tom did not want the job, but, he said, "it would be wrong to decline." So in the fall, Tom took Martha and their two daughters to live in the Governor's Palace in Williamsburg.

For three years General Washington's army had been fighting the British. King George did *not* want to lose his valuable American colonies, so he sent more and more ships with more soldiers and more guns.

The winter of 1777–1778, the British army had stayed warm and dry in New York City while George

General George Washington *(right)* and the French Marquis de Lafayette at Valley Forge, winter of 1777–1778

Washington's army froze and starved in the snowy fields of Valley Forge. Washington had written to Congress that he had "men without clothes . . . without blankets . . . without shoes. . . . " But somehow General Washington managed to keep his army together and even win a victory or two. Now, in 1779, he began to push the British south. British soldiers, warships, and guns headed straight for the coast of Virginia.

The next three years were the worst of Tom's life.

He was not a soldier; he was a writer, a builder, a thinker, a farmer. He was also the wartime governor of the largest state in America, which stretched from the Atlantic Ocean to the Mississippi River. Virginia had one thousand miles of coastline and practically no soldiers or weapons to defend it. The state was almost out of money, and the money it had was almost worthless (a paper bill was said to be worth one oak leaf). People did not want to pay taxes, no one wanted to join the army for longer than two months, and the British were coming!

Virginia needed food and money and guns. Governor Jefferson wrote letters night and day, but all his writing didn't bring help. Even worse, Jefferson not only had to provide for the Virginia army but had to send supplies to Washington's army too.

By 1780 the British were attacking Virginia from the north, south, and east; Indians attacked from the west. The government of Virginia—both the legislature and Governor Jefferson—moved to Richmond to stay ahead of the British. In December, the American traitor Benedict Arnold led twenty-seven British ships and sixteen hundred troops into Virginia's Chesapeake Bay, and British soldiers burned part of Richmond. Virginia's government, including Jefferson and his family, moved farther inland.

Nothing Tom tried worked. The messenger line he organized, with fast riders who could gallop 120 miles in twenty-four hours, didn't bring help. The four thousand guns Tom had found weren't enough and were soon lost anyway. The Virginia militia turned and ran when they saw the enemy; the legislature didn't help; and the people blamed Governor Jefferson for every defeat.

France was trying to help the struggling American army. In April, the French officer Lafayette came to Virginia with one thousand men, but many more soldiers were needed to hold off thousands of British red-coats. An exhausted Governor Jefferson asked George Washington to send help (Virginia is a sinking State, Tom said), but General Washington needed help himself.

And in April, Tom and Martha's newest baby, their fifth child, died.

By June 1781 Virginia was in ruins and the British were after Jefferson and the legislature, who had moved all the way to Charlottesville, just below Monticello. Soldiers under the British colonel Tarleton, who was called "the Hunting Leopard," galloped up the mountain toward Monticello. They hoped to capture Governor Jefferson himself. Tom had enough warning to get his family down the mountain to safety before he leaped onto his horse, with as many papers as he could collect, and escaped. Two slaves, Martin Hemings and Caesar, bravely stayed behind to hide valuable silver before the British arrived.

Colonel Tarleton's men touched nothing at Monticello, but another of Tom's farms was not so fortunate. At Elk Hill, General Cornwallis destroyed all Tom's crops, burned his barns and fences, took his cattle and horses, and cut the throats of the horses that were too young to be useful.

The American army won a stunning victory at York-town, Virginia, in October 1781 with the help of the French. The British army surrendered, and the fighting was over. (The Revolutionary War didn't officially end until the peace treaty was signed in 1783.) But Tom was too discouraged to go to the victory celebration for General Washington. He wrote his apology, saying he was too old and decrepit to attend (he was thirty-eight years old).

The Virginia legislature blamed Thomas Jefferson for all the war problems and demanded an explanation. Jefferson carefully wrote out his reasons for everything he had tried, and in the end received the thanks of the legislature. However, he was so shocked and hurt by this demand that he vowed to spend the rest of his life away from politics. He returned to Monticello and wrote to his cousin Edmund Randolph, "I . . . have retired to my farm, my family and books, from which I think nothing will ever more separate me."

Soon after Tom got home, he received a letter from a French official asking for information on the state of Virginia. Thomas Jefferson was the right man to ask. He knew Virginia upside down and inside out; and what he didn't already have in his notes he set out to find. He asked an explorer to send him the weights of every American animal, "from the mouse to the mammoth." He worked on his book *Notes on the State of Virginia* for months, and included everything from geography, climate, people, animals, laws, history, and money to fossil bones.

All the while, Tom continued to build Monticello. The top of his mountain was a mess, with piles of dusty bricks and muddy boards stacked all around the partly built house. Martha and the house slaves did their best to keep the inside of the house in order, but it must have been hard, with floors going down, walls going up, and plaster and dust covering everything.

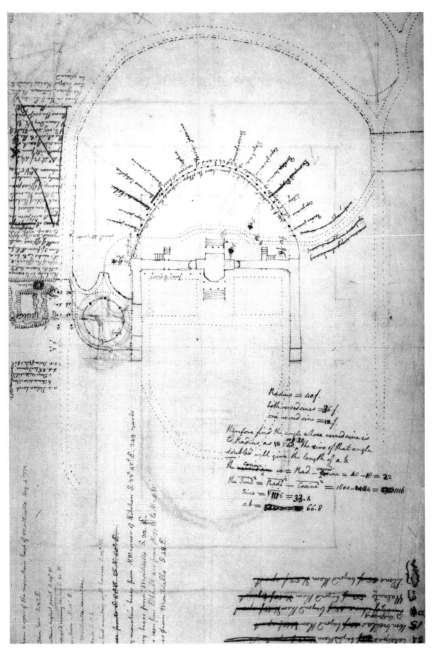

Jefferson's ink drawing of his plan for Monticello, drawn before May 1768. His plans changed over the years.

Monticello was not orderly, and it was not quiet. Shouts of workmen, shrieks of playing children, wails of crying babies, and pounding and hammering filled every disorderly crevice. Ashes and smoke from kitchen fires and the blacksmith's shop drifted silently through the racket.

While Tom supervised the building and farms and planting and wrote every detail and idea into his notebooks, Martha had her own account books. She kept track of the meat and vegetables and wine, and she listed the clothes and food given to each slave. She also did needlework; she made lots of soap and excellent beer; and in the smoky kitchen she read directions out of her cookbook to Ursula, the cook. She supervised the dairy, the cheese and butter making; and she was nurse and doctor to everyone at Monticello, black or white.

The evenings were more peaceful. Tom and Martha even had time to entertain visitors and play the music they loved. After all the problems and sadness they had had, they began to feel happy again. Tom thought 1782 might turn out all right after all.

That spring Tom and Martha's sixth child, Lucy, was born strong and healthy. Tom proudly weighed the baby on the same scales he used to weigh Martha's silk stockings, his silver coffeepot, and the sugar he put in his coffee. But Martha couldn't get out of bed. She became weaker and weaker. Tom moved his writing desk to Martha's bedside and would not leave her. He tried everything he knew to bring Martha back to health and happiness. He played and sang for her; he had only the most tempting food prepared for her; he gave her medicine; he read to her. But Martha died in September.

Tom went into his room and closed the door. He stayed there, alone, for three weeks. There was nothing that Tom's sister Martha or ten-year-old Patsy or four-year-old Polly could do to help. He burned every single paper and letter that belonged to his wife, except for some lines from a book that they copied together just before she died. He put a lock of her auburn hair with that paper, folded it carefully, and locked it away in a secret drawer. His beloved Martha had been "torn from him by Death," and he had those bitter words carved on her gravestone.

When Tom left his room at last, he got on his favorite horse and galloped furiously through the woods on his mountain. Slowly he began to make notes again. Finally, ten weeks later, he wrote to his worried friends about the "stupor" he had been in, and told them he had felt as dead as his wife was. But he had three children, a new country, and things to do.

In the spring of 1783, Tom went to work on his library. He made a list of every one of his 2,640 books and arranged them according to subject. Then he made a list of every slave he owned (204 men, women, and children) and on which of his five farms they lived. Then he made a list of every letter he had ever written, by name and date. At least he had *something* in his control.

Soon Tom was elected as the Virginia delegate to Congress. He took Patsy to Philadelphia, where she would live and go to school while he was with Congress in Annapolis. He wrote Patsy every few days, reminding her how to dress, what to study, and to "never do or say a bad thing." He wrote not only his own wishes, but also what he thought her mother would have taught her.

In November 1783, Tom sent a schedule to eleven-year-old Patsy:

from 8. to 10 o'clock practice music.
from 10. to 1. dance one day and draw another.
from 1. to 2. draw on the day you dance, and write a
    letter the next day.
from 3. to 4. read French.
from 4. to 5. exercise yourself in music.
from 5. till bedtime read English, write &c.

By December he was quite cross, as Patsy was not writing often enough. "I hoped before this to have received letters from you regularly and weekly," he wrote. By April he was even more cross. "I have not received a letter from you since early in February," he wrote stiffly. "This is far short of my injunctions to write once a week by post."

Meanwhile, in Congress, Tom found himself in the midst of constant fussing with a group of lawyers who, Tom said, "question everything, yield nothing, and talk by the hour." The thirteen colonies had become thirteen separate states, each state with its own laws and its own money, and the brand-new country was in danger of falling apart.

Tom began his work in Congress by designing a new system of money for all the United States, based on tens and ones, using pennies, dimes, and dollars. Then within six months he wrote thirty-one important papers that laid the foundation for the new American republic.

In March 1784, the state of Virginia gave its western lands to the government of the United States. Thomas Jefferson wrote the Ordinance of 1784, which included an article stating that after 1800 there would be no slavery in new states made from this land. But again Jefferson had gone too far for Congress, and his idea to contain slavery failed by *one* vote. The fate of millions, Tom wrote sadly, was determined by one man.

5

FRANCE

Jefferson was unhappy with Congress, and he missed his wife terribly. In May 1784, when Congress asked him to go to France to work with John Adams and Benjamin Franklin on trade agreements, he agreed instantly.

Tom bought three tickets. Going with him were twelve-year-old Patsy, who was already tall, auburn-haired, and amiable, just like her father; and James Hemings, a slave who was to learn how to cook the French way. Young Polly and Lucy stayed home with their Aunt Elizabeth Eppes.

On July 5 the Jeffersons sailed out of Boston Harbor on a small, tidy ship named *Ceres*. When they arrived in France after nineteen days at sea, Mr. Jefferson found a house in Paris for himself, and the best school (a Catholic convent) in the city for Patsy. Patsy lived at the school, and Tom visited her every single day for two months (and wrote instructions for her daily schedule) until she was quite happy with her new friends and her new language.

Jefferson's job was to work out agreements to sell

American whale oil, salted fish, rice, and tobacco to the Europeans, so the United States could get started as a new nation. People here, Tom wrote home, know so little about the United States that "we might as well be in the moon." He also took over as minister to France, succeeding the elderly Benjamin Franklin, and plunged into the colorful work of attending the French court as the official representative of the United States government. He did such a good job that he was soon "much beloved," and invited to a dinner or dancing party every night.

Tom chuckled at the sight of thousands of barbers rushing through the streets of Paris carrying curling irons and hair powder (it was unthinkable for a man to comb his own hair). He grumbled about having his own hair fixed every day, and said he just might cut it off. He complained about buying new outfits for every single court occasion.

Tom went to the king's palace at Versailles, rattling down the long cobblestoned drive in his carriage (and a new outfit). There he saw tall mirrors and taller windows; sky blue satin curtains; and walls, chairs, and tables covered with gold. There were 230 bathrooms, and thousands of rooms for sitting, standing, and dancing. Tom bowed politely to the ladies. He tried not to stare at their incredible hairdos, some with sailing ships or vases full of water and flowers sitting on top of a tower of hair, the higher the better.

After seeing Versailles, Mr. Jefferson wrote that he was sure simple American farmers were "the chosen people of God."

Paris had six hundred thousand people, no sidewalks, and no quiet. Day and night there were food sellers shouting; iron wheels and galloping hooves clattering over the cobblestones; and drivers of coaches, farm carts, cabs, and huge gilded carriages screaming at people in the way.

But Paris had bookstores. Tom spent almost every afternoon exploring Paris, buying books and more books. He was a fussy shopper. "I like a fine white paper, neat type and neat binding," he wrote. In other stores he bought ribbons for Patsy and a map, a sword, and lace ruffles for himself. He bought wallpaper, silverware, and furniture for his house in Paris. He bought every new kitchen gadget he saw, and dozens of heavy iron and copper pans to help James with his French cooking.

Tom was just beginning to enjoy Paris when he received dreadful news from Virginia. His two-year-old daughter, Lucy, was dead. He had now lost four of his children to death, and had only two children left, Patsy and Polly. Tom decided that six-year-old Polly must come to Paris so they could be together, and he immediately wrote to her. But Polly didn't want to go to France.

It was cold and wet in Paris that winter, and Tom was sad and lonely. He wrote many letters to his friends at home, and he made notes about the contents of every letter he sent, every day. Tom had done this all his life, but it was very tedious. Then in France he heard about a new invention—a copying press! He instantly ordered one, and from the day it arrived, Tom had to write a finished letter only once.

Jefferson received his first copying machine, invented by James Watt, in 1785 in Paris. To use this Watt press, Jefferson wrote with a special ink, then rolled his original paper and a tissue paper in the press, making a copy on the tissue paper.

He wrote Polly again, saying she must come to France because he and Patsy could not live without her. Polly still did not want to go to Paris.

Tom's good friends John and Abigail Adams had moved to London. So in the spring of 1786, Tom went to cold, wet London to visit them and to see England for himself. In London, Jefferson was presented to his former king, George III, at a royal gathering. King George had not gotten over the rebellion of his colonists, and he rudely turned his back to Jefferson. When Tom next wrote to George Washington he said that while he had been an enemy of kings before, now he was "ten thousand times more so since I have seen what they are."

Meanwhile, Tom had waited two years for Polly to come to Paris, and he was tired of waiting. He wrote Elizabeth that Polly *must* come, whether she wanted to or not. He gave instructions about the right ship to put Polly on, and said the "careful negro woman" who would bring her must be mature and must have had smallpox.

Tom decided to see southern France and Italy before Polly's arrival. He left Patsy in school and drove alone in his carriage with rented horses. Before long, his notebooks overflowed with notes. He wrote about plants that might grow well in America, about conversations he had with farmers, and his thoughts about everything he saw. And, of course, he wrote letters of advice to Patsy. When he received a letter saying she couldn't learn her Greek grammar, he wrote back firmly that an American can "surmount every difficulty." And, just in case Patsy should think of relaxing, he added, "It is wonderful how much may be done if we are always doing."

After seeing France, Italy, Germany, England, and Holland, Jefferson wrote a friend that he would prefer "a very modest cottage with my books, my family, and a few old friends, dining on simple bacon" to the most splendid position on earth.

Soon after Tom returned to Paris, nine-year-old Polly finally arrived. She was not accompanied by a mature woman, as Tom had asked, but by James Hemings's sister, fourteen-year-old Sally. Polly hadn't seen her father or sister since she was five, and at first she didn't even recognize them. But Patsy knew what to do, because Mr. Jefferson had written it down for her. Patsy was to "teach

In 1786, while visiting England, Jefferson sat for this portrait by Mather Brown at the request of John and Abigail Adams. The Adamses bought the painting, and it has remained in the Adams family.

[Polly] above all things to be good. . . . Teach her to be always true. . . . Teach her never to be angry. . . ." Polly was enrolled in Patsy's school and soon was so happy in Paris that she used her French name, Maria, the rest of her life.

Jefferson spent every Sunday with his two daughters. As they drove through Paris the girls talked about their lessons, their books, their music. Mr. Jefferson told them the latest news from home and what he had heard about the new constitution for the United States.

Tom's friend James Madison was helping to write the Constitution, a document that would establish one government over all the states. Tom wrote him that he was worried because there was nothing in the Constitution about the rights of the *people*. Human rights were at least as important as property rights, Tom said.

Meanwhile, the extremes between rich and poor in France were taking a dangerous turn. As Tom rode and walked through the streets of Paris he saw miserable people living on the streets, starving, begging, trying to keep warm over bonfires. "What could be the reason," he wrote to Madison, "that so many should be permitted to beg who are willing to work?" He wrote to his friend James Monroe, "How little do my countrymen know what precious blessings they are in possession of, and which no other people on earth enjoy. I confess I had no idea of it myself."

The winter of 1788–89 was fearfully cold. The poor people of Paris were starving and dying in streets filled with sewage and putrid icy water. When mothers cried for bread outside the palace, one well-fed nobleman said they could eat grass if they were really hungry.

The young French queen, Marie Antoinette, couldn't see any problems. The young French king, Louis XVI, could hardly see anything at all. He was so nearsighted he recognized people only by the sound of their voices, as it was not dignified for a king to wear glasses.

Tom hoped France could change peacefully, but to be safe he wanted to take his daughters back to America. Once they were settled at home he would return to

Jefferson's daughter Patsy, age seventeen, Paris 1789. Jefferson wrote his sister-in-law in 1788 that Patsy had inherited his height, "and that, you know, is inheriting no trifle."

The storming of the Bastille in Paris in 1789 was the beginning of the French Revolution.

his work in France. So in the spring he wrote George Washington, who had just been elected the first president of the United States, and asked for permission to return home.

Before Tom received permission to leave, the French Revolution began—not peacefully. Crowds of angry citizens armed with wooden farm tools tore down the Bastille, a French prison, stone by stone. In this crisis the king's mind, Tom wrote, "was weakness itself."

Thomas Jefferson, his two daughters, James and Sally Hemings, one dog, and a massive pile of trunks and boxes left France in October. In November, they arrived in Virginia. Surprising news awaited.

6

THE FIRST SECRETARY OF STATE

To his shock, Tom learned that George Washington had put forward his name as the first secretary of state for the United States. Tom did not want the job, but how could he refuse? He thought about it on the slow drive through Virginia as he visited with his old friends. He thought about it as his sweating horses trotted up the steep winding road to Monticello. He thought about it when his slaves greeted him with cries and kisses and he was home at last. Tom, now forty-six, had been gone five years.

Tom walked through his house and up and down his garden. He rode slowly over each of his farms. His managers and overseers hadn't done things the way Tom would have. His house and farms were in terrible condition. He wrote President Washington that he couldn't take the job.

After Christmas James Madison, who'd been elected to the House of Representatives, arrived at Monticello from New York, the United States capital. He brought another plea from President Washington, and he told Tom that the general good of America required the best men to serve their country. Finally, in February 1790, Jefferson agreed.

Patsy, all grown up and now called Martha, had found a suitable husband. Tom was pleased, as he had feared "that in marriage she will draw a blockhead." Martha's choice was Thomas Mann Randolph, a cousin who lived not far from Monticello. They were married in February, and it was agreed that they would care for Monticello, and eleven-year-old Polly (called Maria), while Tom was away.

Jefferson disliked arguing and tried to be courteous in every situation, but in New York he was surrounded by fierce disagreement. Some powerful men, including Tom's old and dear friend John Adams, thought the common people should be ruled. Adams, who was vice president, also thought senators should be appointed for life from among the rich landowners. He thought the title "president" much too plain, and even George Washington thought "High Mightiness" wasn't too bad. Tom was horrified. Americans had just gone to a lot of trouble to make a government of the *people*, not of a king.

The secretary of the treasury, Alexander Hamilton, agreed with Adams that the rich and wellborn should rule. People who thought like Adams and Hamilton were called Federalists.

Thomas Jefferson believed in rule by the people, based on education and talent. In fact, Jefferson's belief in the ability of citizens to govern themselves is the soul of American democracy. People who agreed with Jefferson were called Republicans (later called Democrats).

Hamilton and Jefferson were soon in violent disagreement on almost every subject, right down to the clothes

President George Washington and his cabinet *(left to right):* George Washington, Henry Knox (secretary of war), Alexander Hamilton (secretary of the treasury), Thomas Jefferson (secretary of state), and Edmund Randolph (attorney general). Jefferson is the only one not wearing ruffles.

they wore. Hamilton wore fine silk and lace and ruffles. Jefferson wore a simple white shirt and black pants. Some said they were born to hate each other, and it certainly felt that way to Jefferson.

In the midst of these problems, Thomas Jefferson sharpened his quill pens and set to work. As the first secretary of state he was in charge of the post office, the office for inventions, and the office that made the money for the United States. He had to set rules for weighing and measuring for all the states. He had to establish the way the United States would work with other countries, and make peace with the British, Spanish, and Indians—all of whom were on the borders of the new United States.

Immediately after each meeting with President Washington, Jefferson wrote down what they talked about. His notes looked like this: "Sent for by the President. Went. I said . . . He then . . . We should . . . but how? I think . . ."

He wrote to Martha and her husband and to Maria. He wrote to Noah Webster. He wrote to friends all over America and Europe. He wrote to Lafayette in France. He wrote to senators and lawmakers and Indian chiefs.

He wrote piles, masses, heaps of papers and letters.

After being in New York only two months, Tom had such a terrible headache that he could hardly see. He longed to be at Monticello, far from the anger and problems in New York. His headache finally went away, but the war of ideas did not.

The government moved to the new capital city of Philadelphia in the fall of 1790. Mr. Jefferson had all his things from Paris shipped there, since he wouldn't be going back to France, and then he had more problems. There were eighty-six enormous cases of furniture and a huge freight bill to pay ($544.53, he wrote in his account book). There were so many boxes that he couldn't get them all in the house he rented, so he had to pay a storage bill, too. His servants worked as fast as they could, carefully unpacking fifty-nine chairs upholstered in blue and crimson; sofas covered with gold leaf; clocks; draperies;

scientific instruments; boxes of macaroni; a fountain; and much, much more.

Clean and tidy Philadelphia's streets had pebbles down the middle and footpaths of red brick on each side. The houses were also brick, built right up to the sidewalks, and the society was even richer and more fashionable than in New York. President and Mrs. Washington gave parties every week (though President Washington didn't say much), and the high-class ladies of Philadelphia vied with each other to see who could wear the fanciest, tallest hairdo and the most elegant London dress.

Just the way it was when George III owned America, Mr. Jefferson thought sadly.

Jefferson did *not* dress according to London fashion, and he still slouched crookedly in his chair with his long legs sticking out. But his papers and books were always in the neatest order. He always wrote with a sharply trimmed quill, and every line in his notebooks was so meticulously straight and neat that the tiny letters appeared to be made by a miniature printing press—the better to read, he'd say.

Tom's daughter Martha had her first baby in January 1791, and she apologized to her father for not writing more often. She was busy, she wrote, organizing the household at Monticello. She was also taking Maria in hand, but feared Maria had "an astonishing degree" of laziness.

Jefferson wrote his daughters faithfully every week. "On the 27th. of February I saw blackbirds and Robinred breasts," he wrote Maria, "and on the 7th. of this month I heard frogs. Have you noted the first appearance of these things at Monticello?"

He sent Martha advice regarding a problem with a relative. Consider the bad parts of a person as a bad key on the harpsichord, he said. "Do not touch on it, but make yourself happy with the good ones. Every human being, my dear, must thus be viewed . . . for none of us, no not one, is perfect. All we can do," he wrote, "is make the best of our friends: love and cherish what is good in them, and keep out of the way of what is bad. . . ."

And to Maria, he sent a bill for letters due. "Balance due T.J. 4." (Unlike Martha, Maria seldom wrote to her father.)

In 1791 the Bank of the United States was opened, as Alexander Hamilton wished. In 1792 the United States assumed the war debt of each state, as Alexander Hamilton wished. Jefferson did not believe that the national government should collect money from each state for the war debt, since some states, including Virginia and other southern states (and Jefferson personally), had already paid most of their debt in full. But these states, and Jefferson, finally agreed with Hamilton. In exchange, the United States capital would not be Philadelphia or New York in the north, but a new city farther south, on the Potomac River—to be ready for use in about ten years.

When President Washington began his second term, he asked Jefferson to stay on as secretary of state, even though Hamilton had written Washington that Jefferson was "dangerous to the union, peace and happiness of the

Alexander Hamilton and Thomas Jefferson. Both portraits were painted by Charles Willson Peale at approximately the same time in the early 1790s.

country." Jefferson in turn wrote to Washington that Hamilton would "undermine and demolish the republic." Jefferson also told President Washington that he wanted to retire to Monticello, the sooner the better. But Washington did not want him to retire, and Jefferson decided that he could not retreat from battle with Hamilton. He agreed to stay on.

Then horrifying news arrived from France that King Louis XVI and Queen Marie Antoinette had been guillotined. This put Secretary of State Jefferson in an awkward position, because he had supported the French Revolution. Now he argued with Hamilton over what to do about the new French government, which had not only cut off the heads of the French king and queen, but had also declared war on England.

Tom didn't want to argue. He really wanted to go home to Monticello. In July of 1793, he sent a letter of resignation to President Washington. But Washington said he and the country *needed* Jefferson. Reluctantly, Tom agreed once more to stay on as secretary of state.

Jefferson the Republican and Hamilton the Federalist continued to disagree bitterly about everything from banks to voting. Each man was absolutely certain that he and his party were right. Sadly, only fifteen years after the revolution that was to create a new government for all Americans, the United States had two violently different political parties.

President Washington was appalled by this division. He said he would rather be in his grave than in these circumstances. He had worked to make a truly united country with one goal for all; now he worried whether the United States could remain in one piece. Jefferson wasn't the only one who wanted to go home. Washington wanted to return to his farm, too, but he had agreed to serve a second term as president in order to preserve the union. He spoke to Jefferson and Hamilton privately, begging them to make up their differences. They could not.

Finally Jefferson couldn't stand it any longer. He resigned as secretary of state ("Be pleased to accept it," he wrote to President Washington) and left Philadelphia in January 1794.

7

HOME OR POLITICS?

At Monticello the fifty-one-year-old Jefferson felt like a new man. Every morning he jumped out of bed before the sun was up, walked through his gardens, rode over his farms, and wrote notes and lists about what needed to be done and when. His slave Isaac said he could hear Jefferson singing all day long.

Jefferson had decided to build a new house in the neo-classical Italian style—a long, low house with a dome, like one he had seen in Paris. Again the mountaintop was littered with piles of bricks and boards as most of the old house came down and new cellars were dug. In the midst of hammering and dust and demolition and chaos, Tom wrote that he made "tranquillity the object of my life." He would not give up life at Monticello, he said, "for the empire of the universe."

In his first year back at home Jefferson worked furiously. He directed his field slaves to repair fences; restore his wheat, tobacco, and corn fields (plow *around* the mountain instead of up and down, he said); plant more vegetables and berries; and plant 1,157 peach trees lining the road around the mountain (better than fences). "I live

70

on my horse," he wrote, "from morning to night."

Jefferson added a nail factory to Monticello. He taught the teenage slave boys how to make nails and gave bonuses to the best workers. Soon they were noisily making up to ten thousand nails a day, some used to build Monticello and some sold to other builders. Jefferson needed all the money he could get to keep his farms going and feed his family, his slaves, his animals, and his visitors and *their* slaves and horses.

In December 1794 Tom had made a detailed chart in his Farm Book, with pages and pages of information on his slaves. He listed all their names and families, who lived where, and the clothes and supplies they received. "I have . . . to watch for the happiness," he wrote, "of those who labor for mine."

He made notes to himself about how to farm better the next year. He wrote that it would be smart to have all the wheels for every size wagon be of the same size so that if one wheel broke "you may borrow another from any cart or waggon. . . ." He made a note to feed carrots and straw to the cows.

Tom had his hands—and his Garden Book, Farm Book, account book, notebooks, and house—full. Jefferson's two grandchildren (Martha had her second baby in 1793), his daughter Maria, two of his sisters and their families and their slaves were all at Monticello in "every corner of every room." Martha and her husband also stayed at Monticello as often as possible, because Martha managed her father's household in addition to her own.

But as much as Jefferson's family and farms needed

him, his country needed him more. A worn-out President Washington retired to Mount Vernon, and the two political parties, the Federalists and Republicans, jumped into battle. The Republicans wanted Thomas Jefferson to be the next president; the Federalists wanted Vice President John Adams as president. Adams himself thought it only fair that he should follow Washington and become the second president of the United States.

Adams was elected president in November 1796. Jefferson came in second and, because of the law at that time, became vice president.

Jefferson had hoped to arrive in Philadelphia quietly, but he was met by loud, cheering crowds and troops with a banner saying "Jefferson, the Friend of the People." On inauguration day, March 4, 1797, tall Mr. Jefferson had his red hair tied in a queue (ponytail) with a black ribbon, and wore a long blue frock coat for the ceremony in the Senate Chamber. Plump Mr. Adams wore black, with a fancy sword at his side.

Tom sent his best wishes to President Adams "that your administration may be filled with glory and happiness. . . ." But because President Adams did not agree with Vice President Jefferson at all, he rarely spoke to him—best wishes or not.

Tom soon felt useless and lonely in Philadelphia, "doing nothing, and having nothing to do." One of his only duties as vice president was to preside over the Senate. He found no clear rules for doing this, so he wrote the rules. His rule book, *A Manual of Parliamentary Practice,* is still used.

John Adams, Federalist, President of the United States 1797–1801

Meanwhile the French Revolution was spreading, and other rulers in Europe began to worry about losing *their* heads. Jefferson watched in horror when the Federalists, who feared French influence in the United States, passed the Alien and Sedition Acts in the summer of 1798. Under these new laws, unwanted immigrants or anyone who published a story critical of the government could be jailed. Jefferson protested, some newspaper editors who supported him were put in prison, and Jefferson's own mail was opened so the Federalists could see what he was up to.

Vice President Jefferson went home to Monticello in the spring of 1799 and stayed there most of the year— thinking about his country's future and building his house. His house had not been worked on while he was in Philadelphia and had been open at the north end with no roof, all winter. "It seems," he wrote in despair, "as if I should never get it inhabitable." Martha came from her home to feed and house her father's constant crowds of company while frantically trying to keep her children out of the workmen's way, and out of the piles of bricks and boards and nails. Maria, meanwhile, had gotten married. She and her husband moved to another farm.

The century ended with a shocking event. In December 1799 George Washington died. There was no longer a great man to hold the country together—and 1800 was an election year.

Jefferson felt torn in two. He wanted to be at Monticello with his books and his family. But he knew that if he were president, he could fight for his belief in a government by the people and for the people. He decided to run against President Adams.

Adams was in trouble with some members of his own Federalist party because he refused to declare war on France. Adams wanted to be reelected, but he would not do what he thought was wrong. All the Federalists agreed on one thing, however. Thomas Jefferson *must not* become president.

The Federalist newspapers were hysterical in their cries against Jefferson, telling of the disasters that would befall America if he were elected president. There would be civil war across the country, the papers screamed; wealthy women would be murdered in their beds by Jefferson's common people. Because Jefferson insisted

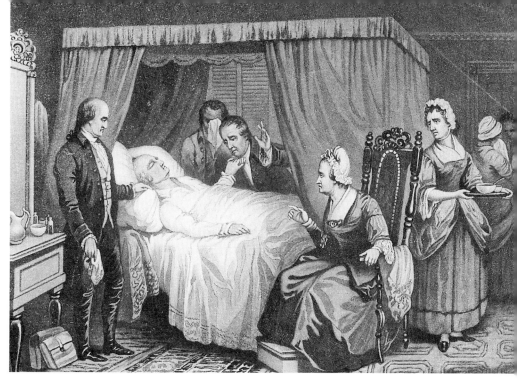

The death of George Washington, 1799. Washington probably died from a combination of strep throat and the medical treatment he was given—draining the blood to get rid of poisons in the body.

on a person's right to freedom of religion, including the freedom to have no religion at all, ministers told their frightened congregations that their Bibles would be taken away and that a vote for Jefferson was a vote against God.

Jefferson stayed at Monticello, building, and did not enter into the ugly, violent arguments between Federalists and Republicans. His friend James Madison and others wrote newspaper articles to present Jefferson's belief in a democracy of the common man.

A few years earlier, Adams and Jefferson had worked together for America's independence; now their two parties fought a bitter and sad battle. When it was over, fifty-seven-year-old Thomas Jefferson had been elected the third president of the United States.

8

PRESIDENT OF THE UNITED STATES

Wednesday, March 4, 1801, was inauguration day for Jefferson and his vice president Aaron Burr in the swampy, muddy new capital city of Washington. The new president did not strap on a shiny sword. He did not ride in a fancy carriage. Jefferson dressed in green breeches, gray stockings, a gray waistcoat, and his best black shoes, and he walked the two blocks from his boardinghouse up the muddy hill to the partly built Capitol building. Riflemen paraded smartly, cannons roared, and cheering people lined the way. Crowds of friends walked with Jefferson, and more crowds waited in the Senate Chamber. But John Adams was too sad and disappointed to watch his former friend become president. He had left Washington the night before.

President Jefferson tried to restore harmony with his inaugural speech. He said that Republicans and Federalists should "unite with one heart and one mind." He spoke

Thomas Jefferson, President of the United States 1801–1809. Painting by Gilbert Stuart

about the ideas and hopes that Americans *shared*, rather than their differences.

After the inauguration, President Jefferson returned to the boardinghouse for dinner. He stayed there for two more weeks, paying fifteen dollars a week for bed and meals, until the President's House was ready.

Although he didn't have an office, President Jefferson set to work immediately. He freed all those who had been put in prison under the Alien and Sedition Acts, and he chose his friend the brilliant James Madison to be secretary of state.

When Jefferson finally moved into the President's House, it still was not finished. The house was built of sandstone, painted white, and had twenty-three rooms. But the roof leaked, the bedrooms were not painted, and the East Room wasn't plastered. Fortunately Jefferson was used to living in an unfinished house.

He had the trash hauled away from the overgrown lawns, a rail fence put up, and the leaky roof replaced, and he designed two low wings to be built on each side of the house. The president's office had a long table in the center, with fourteen chairs. President Jefferson immediately filled the room with books, pull-down maps, globes, his writing desk, a new polygraph, and carpentry and gardening tools. He had roses and geraniums growing at the windows, and he had a pet mockingbird ("a superior being in the form of a bird," he said) with a beautiful song.

President Jefferson got up every morning at five o'clock. He wrote and read government papers and met with important officials until noon. Then he took a long

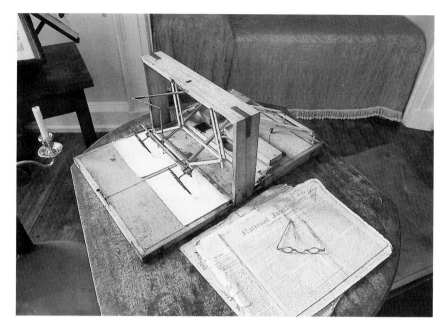

Jefferson's polygraph and reading glasses. Jefferson acquired his first polygraph, a new copying device, in 1804. A polygraph had two pens connected together, two pieces of paper, and two ink pots. When Jefferson wrote with one pen, the other pen made a copy. He liked this device so much (and it broke so often) that he used at least twelve different polygraphs in the next twenty-two years.

horseback ride, wearing round green sunglasses on bright sunny days. On special occasions only, he used a carriage with four perfectly matched bay horses. After the ride came afternoon dinner, with eight to eighteen guests at Jefferson's big, round table. He was back at his writing desk by six o'clock in the evening, and wrote until bedtime. Out of twenty-four hours, he said, he had only "4 hours for riding, dining & a little unbending."

Jefferson wrote all his own letters, all his own speeches, and all his own state papers. He tried glass pens for writing, but didn't like them as well as quills, so he bought three hundred quill pens. He also bought hundreds of sheets of paper and countless bottles of ink.

Jefferson wrote his college friend John Page that he wanted government finances to be as simple to understand as those of the ordinary farmer. Making finances simple was not simple, but President Jefferson reduced taxes *and* paid off some of the country's debt. He also refused all gifts and honors, and all attention, as much as possible. When Massachusetts farmers gave him a giant 1,660-pound cheese made with the milk of nine hundred cows, he insisted on paying them two hundred dollars. "The whole art of government," Jefferson said, "consists in the art of being honest."

President Jefferson invited groups of Federalists to dine with him several times a week for "the holy cause of freedom," so they could resolve their differences calmly, with common sense and courtesy. Jefferson's dinners were famous—they had the most delicious French cooking, the best wines, and the most brilliant conversation in the United States. He had his own recipe for ice cream, which he had his French chef make almost every day. He put new and strange things on his round mahogany dinner table, such as pancakes (panne-quaiques, as his French cook spelled it), macaroni, and foods flavored with vanilla.

Jefferson did not have special seating for special people at his table (that's why it was round), but some people were insulted when they were not given privileged treatment. President Jefferson did not even bow—he shook hands! This was too much equality for the Federalists, who found fault with every act of the new president. They *did* go to his dinners, though.

The Federalists hoped that Jefferson's openness would be his downfall. It wasn't. In fact, John Adams's own son, John Quincy Adams, said that Jefferson's ideas were "popular in all parts of the nation." The Federalists poured their rage and frustration into the newspapers, trying to divide Americans and weaken Jefferson's presidency.

Jefferson's enemies were delighted with a story that was published in a Federalist newspaper. The story was written by James Callender, who wanted the job of postmaster of Richmond, Virginia, and whom Jefferson had *not* hired. Callender wrote that Sally Hemings, the young slave who had accompanied Maria to Paris, was Jefferson's secret lover and that he was the father of five of her children. President Jefferson did not respond at all to Callender's story, except to tell his friends privately that it was not true.

When Jefferson became president, Spain was interfering with American ships and their goods on the Mississippi River at New Orleans, where the river flowed into the Gulf of Mexico. At first President Jefferson believed the city of New Orleans belonged to the Spanish. He soon discovered, however, that Spain had turned New Orleans and the rest of the Louisiana Territory, the land between the Mississippi River and the Rocky Mountains, over to the French. Jefferson sent James Monroe to talk with the French emperor, Napoleon, about buying New Orleans so American ships could safely use the Mississippi River.

Jefferson's timing couldn't have been better. Napoleon was worried about a possible war with England, and France needed money more than it needed a piece of a faraway continent. To Jefferson's surprise, Napoleon decided to sell not only New Orleans, but the entire Louisiana Territory to the United States. So for fifteen million dollars, in 1803, President Jefferson bought it all.

No one (except the Indians who lived there) knew what this new land was like. No one even knew how big it really was. But Jefferson could hardly wait to find out. He

LOUISIANA PURCHASE
(1803)

chose his talented secretary, Meriwether Lewis, to lead the exploration of this huge new part of the United States. Lewis chose William Clark as his partner, and they began to prepare for the journey.

"The object of your mission," Jefferson wrote to Lewis and Clark, "is to explore the Missouri river" in order to find a waterway to the Pacific Ocean. President Jefferson wrote pages and pages of instructions about drawings to make and facts to learn about this new land and everything in and on it. He warned them to make several copies of their notes and to be sure that one copy was on birch bark, as water wouldn't hurt it as much.

In May 1804, Lewis and Clark, along with forty-five men and a dog, set off from St. Louis in three boats, paddling upstream on the Mississippi under a dark gray sky.

President Jefferson did not see them off. In April he had rushed from Washington to Monticello, where twenty-five-year-old Maria lay weak and pale with her new baby. He arrived only in time to kiss his daughter before she died.

After Maria died, Jefferson sat alone in his room, with his Bible open on his knee. He wrote to his old friend John Page, "I . . . have lost . . . half of all I had."

Jefferson returned to Washington alone. It was a terrible trip. The pouring rain matched his grief-filled mood. His horse "got into ill temper and refused" to pull the carriage through the deep, sloppy mud. At last President Jefferson unhitched the horse and rode the fifty-five miles to Washington.

Jefferson ran for president again in 1804 and won an

overwhelming victory (even John Adams voted for him). Jefferson had doubled the size of the United States without a war or firing a shot. He had reduced the national debt, cut taxes, and kept America at peace. This time his vice president was George Clinton because Aaron Burr, his first vice president, had fled west after killing Alexander Hamilton in a duel.

In September 1806 Lewis and Clark returned to St. Louis. They had not found a waterway to the Pacific Ocean, because there isn't one, but they had explored

The Lewis and Clark expedition at the Celilo Falls on the Columbia River. From a mural in Oregon's state capitol rotunda at Salem

from the Mississippi River to the Pacific Ocean. They had walked or paddled their canoes more than seven thousand miles and collected samples of everything they saw. Only one man died on the entire two-year journey, and that was from appendicitis. The expedition was a tremendous success.

President Jefferson, however, was having problems in Washington. In November 1806 the British, who were at war with France, began trying to capture and board every American ship on the Atlantic. The British said they were looking for British sailors on American ships. They also wanted to stop America from helping France.

In response, Jefferson—who had a "passion for peace"—declared a trade embargo against England, which meant any trade with that country was forbidden. He expected Americans to buy from Americans instead of from England. But Jefferson's embargo did not work because American business needed the trade with England, and the blockade made many Americans angry at President Jefferson. Hateful letters and cartoons appeared in the newspapers.

Even though Jefferson was disappointed with what he believed were lies in the newspapers, he believed in the newspapers' right to print them. He suggested, however, that newspapers should have four chapters: the first chapter for the truth; the second for probabilities; the third for possibilities; and the fourth for lies. "The first chapter would be very short," he said.

President Jefferson's grandson Jeff had trouble keeping his temper when folks critized his grandfather. In a letter to Jeff, the president wrote, "When I hear another express an opinion which is not mine, I say to myself, He has a right to his opinion, as I to mine. . . . It is his affair, not mine, if he prefers error." Jefferson advised his grandson to stay in good humor and treat rude people kindly, as if they were sick patients in need of medical treatment.

President Jefferson's second term continued to go badly. He tried to buy Florida from Spain, but Spain wouldn't sell. His former vice president, Aaron Burr, was trying to persuade the western states to separate from the union and elect him their president. Burr was arrested, but freed by a Federalist judge against Jefferson's wishes. By this time Jefferson could hardly wait for retirement so he could serve America in other ways.

Jefferson's friend James Madison became the fourth president of the United States in March 1809. At the inaugural ball, the windows blazed with bayberry candles, dance music filled the room, and Jefferson was, he said, the happiest man at the party.

A few days later sixty-five-year-old Thomas Jefferson left Washington in a snowstorm, heading straight for Monticello. The snow was so deep that his carriage got stuck in a snowdrift, but that didn't stop him. He jumped on one of the horses and rode for eight hours through blinding snow until he reached his favorite spot on earth.

9

MONTICELLO

At last Thomas Jefferson was home to stay, and the great new house he had begun years before was finished. (Or, as his slave Isaac said, he stopped building. It was never really finished.) He wrote to an old friend that Monticello was where his happiness began and ended.

Jefferson had drawn all the plans, measured all the walls, and shown his bricklayers exactly what he wanted. He had chosen the paint for the walls. He had chosen the fabric for the draperies and the pictures for hanging. He had drawn plans for flower beds and walking paths. He had hired the best blacksmiths, carpenters, and bricklayers he could afford, and had his most talented slaves work with them.

A forest covered the entire mountain except for the top. Bridle paths, carriage paths, and footpaths ran up and down and around, through the lilacs, redbuds, dogwoods, and maples. At the very top, looking down onto the Blue Ridge Mountains, was Jefferson's house. His huge garden, on the sunny south side of the mountain, was eighty feet

West front of Monticello. The fishpond in the foreground was built in 1808.

wide and one thousand feet (one-fifth of a mile) long. Below the garden were even larger orchards and vineyards.

Mulberry Row, between the house and the garden, was the workshop area of Monticello. There was a building where the slaves wove cloth; a washhouse; a smokehouse; a dairy where butter and cream were made; a metalworking shop; a blacksmith and nailery shop; a stable; and a woodworking shop in which black and white carpenters worked together.

Also on Mulberry Row were five log cabins for the slaves who did the cooking, washing, housecleaning, sewing, and child tending for the large Jefferson family. Martha and her eleven children (and sometimes her husband) lived at Monticello now, along with Tom's sister Martha and her children, and many other relatives, some with children, some without.

Jefferson's nine house slaves, mainly from the large Hemings family, wore formal clothes. They fetched and carried for the Jefferson family, built fires, set the table, met the guests, did the errands, and carried money.

Two long extended brick wings built into the hillsides stretched out from Jefferson's house. In the south wing were white-painted rooms with fireplaces where the cook and the house slaves lived, the kitchen, a smoke room, and the dairy. The north wing had stables, a carriage house, a laundry, and an icehouse. The icehouse, Monticello's refrigerator, was a huge hole in the ground, lined with stone and hay and filled with sixty-two wagonloads of ice from the Rivanna River. The two wings were connected to the main house by a great brick cellar stocked with wood, food, coffee, and wine.

Jefferson's house had three stories. The top floor was for helpers and anyone who didn't fit into the other twenty-three rooms. In the very center of the top floor was the dome room, with huge round windows all around and a round glass skylight on top—the first skylight in the United States. The second floor was filled with small bedrooms for grandchildren and visitors. The first floor of Monticello was for the Jefferson family adults and special guests such as James and Dolley Madison, who often visited from their farm twenty-six miles away (when they

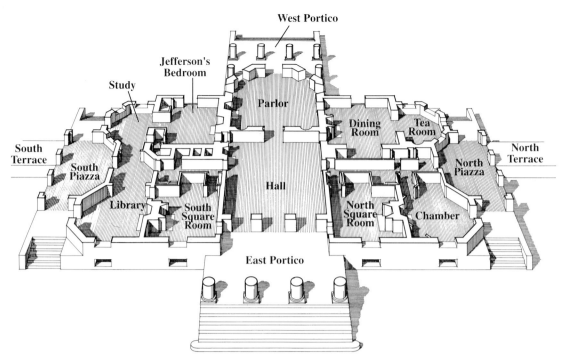

Floor plan of the first floor of the finished Monticello. Jefferson wanted his visitors to learn all they could about America, so the hall was like a museum. It was filled with maps, prints, antlers, bones, Indian artifacts, and objects from Lewis and Clark.

weren't living in the President's House in Washington).

The front entry of the house had tall glass folding doors that opened into a room decorated with elk antlers, poisoned lances, a painted buffalo robe, and other treasures from Lewis and Clark's explorations. There were ten-thousand-year-old mastodon bones from Kentucky. The walls were covered with maps, including the map of Virginia made by Tom's father, and engravings of the Declaration of Independence. Twenty-eight chairs stood in rows on a grass-green floor for all the visitors waiting to see Mr. Jefferson.

Grand houses usually had grand staircases, but not Monticello. Jefferson thought they were a waste of space and looked too royal. Instead he built two very narrow, steep, winding staircases, one on each side of the house.

Grand *windows* were important, though. Jefferson designed tall windows that let the sunshine pour in, and hung tall mirrors on the walls to reflect it. He put candles in front of the mirrors to double the candlelight at night, which saved money on candles. Other walls were covered with pictures of American buildings and world statesmen, scientists, and explorers.

Jefferson had his own private area, which included his study, bedroom, library, and sitting room. No one entered those rooms without his permission—they were the only place at Monticello where he could be alone, for Mr. Jefferson was overwhelmed with people.

Friends, family, artists, lawyers, priests, congressmen, and perfect strangers swarmed over Monticello. Jefferson's grandson Jeff said people stood and stared at Thomas Jefferson as if he were "a lion in a menagerie." One rude woman even broke a window with her parasol in order to see him better. Families arrived in their carriages, demanding the right to see their former president and expecting to stay for days and weeks.

Jefferson's farm manager said there were so many visitors that the horse stalls were always full. The horses required a wagonload of hay each night, and the visitors themselves ate more than a side of beef a day. Martha felt quite frantic when she had to find beds for fifty people, but like her father she was calm and cheerful on the outside.

Jefferson was certainly not alone at breakfast. Often there were twenty people with him, eating muffins, corn

Jefferson's study had six wooden filing cabinets neatly packed with thousands of letters and bills, all in alphabetical order. He put his polygraph on the writing table, with a comfortable chair and revolving bookstand next to it. His library was just next door, its shelves filled with seven thousand books in seven different languages. He even had an indoor toilet, but no running water.

bread, cold ham, and hot pancakes served by the house slaves. For afternoon dinner there were more guests and much more food: pigeon soup, boiled beef, chicken custard, peas, asparagus, ice cream, and wine. Instead of having one big table taking up space, Jefferson had eight small mahogany tables that could be put together to make a larger and larger table, depending on the number of guests.

Between these large, social meals, Jefferson would escape from his guests. He still wrote every day. After breakfast he worked quietly at his desk, writing to scientists, gardeners, statesmen, neighbors, friends, and strangers, while the sun warmed his shoulders or the rain beat against the windows. He saw himself as being *of use* to America.

Every day the post boy rode up the hill with a heavy bag of letters filled with long and detailed questions for Mr. Jefferson. These letters, Jefferson said, were "all to be answered with due attention and consideration." Soon he was spending hours every day looking up information or just thinking about a problem. Then he took his pen and wrote a detailed, polite, elegant response, no matter how stiff and tired his fingers were. He earnestly and faithfully responded to hundreds of letters a month from people whose names, he said, "I have never before heard." He wrote to John Adams that kind letters require kind answers—but the life of a cabbage would be better than this.

After dinner, Jefferson inspected his gardens and workshops, and rode horseback from farm to farm until dark. He carried everything he needed in his pockets: a pocketknife with twelve tiny tools, an ivory ruler, steel scissors, a goose quill toothpick, keys, and a notebook and pencil.

On summer evenings Jefferson walked along the flower beds bordering the lawn, with a long train of children (Martha's eleven, Maria's two, nieces and nephews, cousins and more) following him. They would play games or run races or simply sit on the lawn under the trees. On winter evenings the family sat inside by the fire and read by candlelight. One candle was enough to read by, Jefferson said, and four were splendid. In the half hour after the sun set and before the candles were brought in, they told riddles and played memory games like "I love my love with an apple. I love my love with an apple and a butterfly. I love my love with an apple and a butterfly and a chocolate. I love . . ."

Jefferson had always spent more as a public official than he had ever earned as a public official, and said that he retired "with hands as clean as they are empty." He had paid his own and his father-in-law's debts, in some cases two and three times over because of devalued money and Hamilton's war debt assumption plan. As a favor he had co-signed a friend's bill for twenty thousand dollars. The friend could not pay, and it became Jefferson's debt instead. Meanwhile, visitors came to Monticello in swarms and stayed for weeks. They and their horses and slaves were fed, and Jefferson sank deeper into debt.

And it wasn't just the visitors. Jefferson's huge family made life very expensive. In fact, counting the slaves,

The first vegetable garden at Monticello was planted in 1774. In 1809 Jefferson had his mountainside leveled out for this long, long garden. The Mulberry Row workshops and cabins ran along the top of the hill in the foreground.

more people (170) lived at Monticello than lived in the nearby city of Charlottesville. There were also 178 hogs, 149 sheep, 71 cattle, 18 horses, 8 mules, and uncounted chickens, rabbits, dogs, and cats.

In 1812 the United States had again declared war on the British. This time the United States wanted England to stop interfering with American ships. A peace treaty was signed in December 1814, but there was no real winner. They just stopped fighting.

During the war the British burned several buildings in Washington, including the President's House and the Library of Congress, the official library of the United

States. In April 1815 Jefferson sold his entire library of priceless books on every subject known to the Library of Congress for $23,950 so that it could begin anew—and to help pay his debts. But, looking sadly at his empty shelves not long after the last of the ten wagons loaded with his books rumbled down the mountain, Jefferson wrote to John Adams, "I cannot live without books." And he bought more.

Jefferson sold some of his slaves for money to pay his debts, but the more he owed, the more he needed slave labor. As much as he disliked the idea of slavery, Jefferson freed only a few of his own slaves. He chose those who could find work, such as James Hemings, the cook who had gone with him to Paris.

In spite of his money problems, Jefferson continued to try out new ideas. He experimented with hundreds of vegetables and fruits (he ate very little meat). He grew plants from Europe, and corn, beans, and other plants brought back by Lewis and Clark. He counted the number of peas it took to make a pint (2,500 peas), so he would know how many rows of peas to plant each spring. He experimented with his cows to learn how they would give the most milk. He raised different kinds of sheep to learn which gave the best wool. And he shared everything he learned, to improve the lives of Americans.

Then Jefferson decided to build a whole university.

"If a nation expects to be ignorant and free," he wrote, "it expects what never was and never will be." In 1817, Jefferson wrote a plan for education in Virginia. His plan included elementary schools, to be within one day's ride

NEW YORK

PENNSYLVANIA

MARYLAND

2

NEW JERSEY

DELAWARE

3

3

4

WEST VIRGINIA
(part of Va.
until 1863)

7, 8

9

10

6

11

5

VIRGINIA

1

1. *New York City*
(First U.S. capital)

2. *Philadelphia*
(Second U.S. capital)

3. *Washington*
(Third U.S. capital)

4. *Annapolis*

5. *Williamsburg*

6. *Richmond*

7. *Charlottesville*

8. *University of Virginia*

9. *Monticello*

10. *Shadwell*

11. *Tuckahoe*

JEFFERSON'S AMERICAN WORLD

of any student, and free of charge; then schools for older students training in professions, sciences, and languages; and finally, university. In 1819 the state of Virginia agreed to spend fifteen thousand dollars for a university.

The University of Virginia was the crowning achievement of Jefferson's life and has been called "possibly the greatest piece of architecture in America." He measured the grounds with his folding ruler and drew all the plans; he designed the buildings, the students' rooms, the lawns; he chose the trees and flowers, the teachers and the subjects they would teach; he provided the library. He even recommended a diet for the students—mainly vegetables. The university opened in 1825.

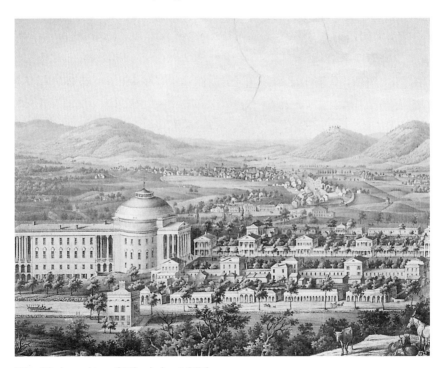

The University of Virginia, 1856

By 1826 Jefferson owed over one hundred thousand dollars, which he could not pay. He continued to welcome friends and strangers to his home and table, even though his chairs now had holes in them, because he felt it was his duty—but he worried about his debts day and night. Finally he wrote a letter to his friend James Madison asking for help. Perhaps there could be a public lottery to raise money?

The lottery was not successful, but Americans responded in other ways. Meetings were held, money was raised. Jefferson's two grandsons paid what they could. None of it was enough to pay off Jefferson's debts, but it was enough to ease his heart.

In 1826 Thomas Jefferson was eighty-three years old. For the first time in his life he was very sick, and he knew he would not get better. "When I can neither read nor ride," he had said, "I shall desire very much to make my bow [to die]." In June he laid down his quill pen for the last time. But he wanted to see one special day in July.

The Fourth of July, 1826, was the fiftieth anniversary of the Declaration of Independence. On the Fourth of July, 1826, Thomas Jefferson died at Monticello.

The last portrait of Thomas Jefferson, painted at Monticello in 1821 by Thomas Sully

LEGACY

Thomas Jefferson collected, in his books and in his mind, the wisdom of the world's great civilizations. He rearranged all he learned, subtracted the impractical and the unjust, added his own brilliant thinking, and created a vision for a new country—the United States of America. Much of the foundation upon which our nation is built came from the mind and the pen of this one man.

Jefferson controlled his life and his emotions with order and reason. He weighed, measured, counted, alphabetized, and fit every scrap of knowledge into an orderly system. He tested every new idea. He squeezed the last drop of information from every subject.

He believed in God, in a planned and orderly universe, and in life after death. But he also believed that "God hath created the mind free." People must be free to not worship God at all, if they so choose.

Thomas Jefferson knew more about every subject from architecture to zoology than any American who lived before him. He probably knew more than any American since. In 1962 President John F. Kennedy told a group of forty-nine Nobel laureates, "I think this is the most extraordinary collection of talent, of human knowledge, that has ever been gathered at the White House—with the possible exception of when Thomas Jefferson dined alone."

Jefferson asked to be remembered for three things he believed he had given Americans. The first represented freedom; the second, worship; and the third, education. As he asked, his gravestone reads:

Here was buried Thomas Jefferson
Author of the
Declaration of American Independence
of the
Statute of Virginia for Religious Freedom
and Father of the
University of Virginia

NOTES

Page 13
Very little is known about Jefferson's brother, Randolph. He apparently lived at Monticello under Tom's care all his life.

Page 21
American English has changed since the 1700s. Jefferson used different spelling than we do. He spelled says, "sais"; payable, "paiable"; steak, "stake."

Page 25
The Virginia House of Burgesses was similar to modern state legislatures.

Page 30
It was said that Sally Hemings was the child of Betty Hemings and Mr. Wayles. If so, Sally Hemings, a slave, would have been the half sister of Tom's wife and the half aunt of his children.

Page 42
Freedom of religion was so important to Jefferson that in 1779 he introduced the "Bill for Establishing Religious Freedom" to the Virginia House of Delegates (formerly House of Burgesses). In the bill Jefferson said, "Almighty God hath created the mind free." The House finally passed the bill in 1786, while Jefferson was in Paris.

Page 57
James and Sally Hemings both received wages in Paris.

Page 63
In 1793, when Thomas Jefferson was secretary of state, these were the Americans who could vote: white men with property. These were the Americans who could *not* vote: white men without property, slaves, children, idiots, and women.

Page 75
In 1800 the United States had sixteen states and five million people—one million of whom were slaves.

Page 76
When Jefferson was inaugurated as president in 1801, Chief Justice John Marshall, another bitter Federalist, turned his back on the president-elect while administering the oath of office to him.

Page 76
When they were old men, Jefferson and Adams became friends again. Mr. Adams wrote to Mr. Jefferson in 1812: "You and I ought not to die before We have explained ourselves to each other." They wrote over 150 letters to each other and saved them all. They wrote about American Indians, Napoleon, science, the nature of man, death, and sadness. They wrote about meeting again after death. They compared the numbers of grandchildren each had, and how far each man could walk and ride in a day. Mr. Adams wrote more often than Jefferson could answer, and said, "Never mind, if I write four letters to your one, your one is worth more than four of mine."

Page 78
John and Abigail Adams had lived in the unfinished President's House for the final two months of Adams's presidency, without stairs and without enough wood for the fireplaces.

Page 80
Jefferson was not a feminist. In 1807 he wrote, "The appointment of a woman to office is an innovation for which the public is not prepared, nor am I."

Page 94
In 1811 Mr. Jefferson wrote down twelve rules of life for his twelve-year-old granddaughter Cornelia:

1. Never put off till tomorrow what you can do today.
2. Never trouble another with what you can do yourself.
3. Never spend your money before you have it.
4. Never buy a thing you do not want because it is cheap; it will be dear [expensive] to you.
5. Take care of your cents; dollars will take care of themselves.
6. Pride costs us more than hunger, thirst, and cold.
7. We never repent of having eaten too little.
8. Nothing is troublesome that one does willingly.
9. How much pain hath cost us the evils which have never happened.
10. Take things always by their smooth handles.
11. Think as you please, and so let others, and you will have no disputes.
12. When angry count to 10 before you speak; if very angry, 100.

Page 94
Although Congress had given the French patriot Lafayette $100,000 in 1824 for his services during the American Revolution, Jefferson was never given a penny beyond his salary.

Page 95
After the War of 1812 the President's House was painted white to cover the scorch marks left when it was burned by the British. Then it became known as the White House.

Page 96

Jefferson was opposed to slavery, but he was a slave owner. Some people believe he had children with a slave woman. Other people believe he did not, but whatever the truth is, Jefferson was caught in the web of slavery.

He made several attempts to change the laws and end slavery. He proposed the idea of freeing all slaves, training them to be self-sufficient, and then deporting them from Virginia—to the West or even back to Africa. All his attempts were defeated. Finally he turned from trying to end slavery to trying to reform it, and hoped the next generation would end slavery.

In 1820, after Missouri entered the union as a slave state, there were eleven slave states and eleven free states. Jefferson saw the horrid possibility of war between the states. "I tremble for my country," he said, "when I reflect that God is just."

Page 99

John Adams died on the very same day as Thomas Jefferson, July 4, 1826.

Page 99

When Thomas Jefferson died, Abraham Lincoln was seventeen years old, Charles Dickens was fourteen, and Karl Marx was eight.

Page 99

Monticello and all Jefferson's possessions, including the slaves, were sold soon after his death.

BIBLIOGRAPHY

Books:

Adams, William Howard. *Jefferson's Monticello.* New York: Abbeville Press, 1983.

Allison, John M. *Adams and Jefferson: Story of a Friendship.* Norman, Oklahoma: University of Oklahoma Press, 1966.

Alsop, Susan Mary. *Yankees at the Court: The First Americans in Paris.* New York: Doubleday & Company, Inc., 1982.

Baron, Robert C., ed. *The Garden and Farm Books of Thomas Jefferson.* Golden, Colorado: Fulcrum, 1987.

Bear, James A., Jr., ed. *Jefferson at Monticello.* Charlottesville: University Press of Virginia, 1967, 1988.

Bedini, Silvio A. *Thomas Jefferson: Statesman of Science.* New York: Macmillan, 1990.

Betts, Edwin Morris, and James Adam Bear, Jr., eds. *The Family Letters of Thomas Jefferson.* Charlottesville: University Press of Virginia, 1966, 1986.

Boardman, F.W. *America and the Virginia Dynasty, 1800–1825.* New York: Henry Z. Walck, 1974.

*Bober, Natalie. *Thomas Jefferson: Man on a Mountain.* New York: Atheneum, 1988.

Boorstin, Daniel J. *The Lost World of Thomas Jefferson.* Boston: Beacon Press, 1948.

Bowers, Claude. *Jefferson in Power.* Boston: Houghton Mifflin, 1936.

Brodie, Fawn. *Thomas Jefferson: An Intimate History.* New York: W. Norton, 1974.

Burstein, Andrew. *The Inner Jefferson.* Charlottesville: University Press of Virginia, 1995.

Cappon, Lester J. *The Adams-Jefferson Letters: Complete Correspondence.* 2 vols. Chapel Hill: Institute of Early American History and Culture, University of North Carolina Press, n.d.

*Crisman, Ruth. *Thomas Jefferson: Man with a Vision.* New York: Scholastic Press, 1992.

Cunningham, Noble E., Jr. *In Pursuit of Reason: The Life of Thomas Jefferson.* New York: Ballantine Books, 1987.

Eames, Charles. *The World of Franklin and Jefferson.* Los Angeles: G. Rice, 1976.

Flexner, James Thomas. *Washington: The Indispensable Man.* Boston: Little, Brown and Co., 1969.

Jefferson, Thomas. *Autobiography.* New York: Heritage Press, 1967.

Jefferson, Thomas. *Notes on the State of Virginia.* Edited by William Peden. Chapel Hill: University of North Carolina Press, 1955.

Lewis, Jan. *The Pursuit of Happiness: Family and Values in Jefferson's Virginia.* London: Cambridge University Press, 1983.

Malone, Dumas. *Jefferson and His Time.* 6 vols. Boston: Little, Brown and Co., 1948–81.

McLaughlin, Jack. *Jefferson and Monticello: The Biography of a Builder.* New York: Henry Holt, 1988.

*Meltzer, Milton. *Thomas Jefferson: The Revolutionary Aristocrat.* New York: Franklin Watts, 1991.

Miller, John Chester. *The Federalist Era.* New York: Harper, 1960.

Miller, John Chester. *The Wolf by the Ears: Thomas Jefferson and Slavery.* New York: New American Library, 1977.

*Morris, Jeffrey. *The Jefferson Way.* Minneapolis: Lerner Publications Co., 1994.

Nichols, Frederick D., and James A. Bear, Jr. *Monticello: A Guidebook.* Monticello, Virginia: Thomas Jefferson Memorial Foundation, 1993.

Onuf, Peter S., ed. *Jeffersonian Legacies.* Charlottesville: University Press of Virginia, 1993.

Padover, Saul K. *Jefferson: A Great American's Life and Ideas.* New York: New American Library, 1952.

*Patterson, Charles. *Thomas Jefferson.* New York: Franklin Watts, 1987.

Peterson, Merrill D. *The Jefferson Image in the American Mind.* New York: Oxford University Press, 1962.

Peterson, Merrill D., ed. *The Portable Thomas Jefferson.* New York: Penguin Books, 1975, 1981.

Randall, Willard S. *Thomas Jefferson: A Life.* New York: Henry Holt & Co., 1993.

Randolph, Sarah N. *The Domestic Life of Thomas Jefferson.* New York: Harper, 1871.

Scheer, George F. *Rebels and Redcoats.* New York: New American Library, 1957.

Stein, Susan R. *The Worlds of Thomas Jefferson at Monticello.* New York: Harry N. Abrams Inc., 1993.

Whitman, Willson, ed. *Jefferson's Letters.* Eau Claire, Wisconsin: E.M. Hale Co., n.d.

Articles:

"Thomas Jefferson." *Cobblestone: The History Magazine for Young People* 10, no. 9 (September 1989).

"Thomas Jefferson." *The Young People's Library of Historical Briefs* (1975).

"Thomas Jefferson's Monticello." *The Magazine Antiques* 144 (July 1993).

Interviews with Author:

Cunningham, Noble E., Jr., Jeffersonian scholar. University of Missouri, 1995.

Stanton, Lucia C., Director of Research. Monticello, 1993.

Stein, Susan, Curator. Monticello, 1993.

*A star denotes a book for younger readers.

All quotations in this biography were taken from the above sources.

INDEX

ACKNOWLEDGMENTS

Illustrations are reproduced through the courtesy of: National Archives, photo no. W&C #66, p. 2; Delaware Art Museum, p. 6; Monticello/Thomas Jefferson Memorial Foundation, pp. 12, 29, 90; The Library of Virginia, print #11803, neg. #A-9-1671, p. 15; Library of Congress, pp. 17, 36, 39, 61, 64, 100; Archive Photos, pp. 20, 39 (inset), 40, 75, front cover; Massachusetts Historical Society, pp. 22, 24, 48; © Kenneth Garrett, p. 37; National Archives photo no. W&C #36, p. 44; Science Museum/Science & Society Picture Library, p. 56; Corbis, p. 58; Diplomatic Reception Rooms, U.S. Department of State, p. 60; Independence National Historical Park, pp. 68 (both), front cover (inset); National Archives photo no. 148-CD-4-15, p.73; Bowdoin College Museum of Art, Brunswick, Maine, Bequest of James Bowdoin III, p. 77; © Buddy Mays/Travel Stock, pp. 79, 92; Oregon State Highway Department, photo #3295, p. 84; Charlottesville Ablemarle Convention and Visitors Bureau, p. 88; © Robert Perron, p. 95; Special Collections, University of Virginia Library, ACC or neg. #RG5/7/2.762 #2028, p. 98.